Griff

THE AUTOBIOGRAPHY OF
TERRY GRIFFITHS

Griff

THE AUTOBIOGRAPHY OF
TERRY GRIFFITHS

WITH JULIAN WORTHINGTON

PELHAM BOOKS
Stephen Greene Press

PELHAM BOOKS/Stephen Greene Press

Published by the Penguin Group
27 Wrights Lane, London W8 5TZ, England
Viking Penguin Inc., 40 West 23rd Street, New York, New York 10010, USA
The Stephen Greene Press, 15 Muzzey Street, Lexington, Massachusetts 02173, US
Penguin Books Australia Ltd, Ringwood, Victoria, Australia
Penguin Books Canada Ltd, 2801 John Street, Markham, Ontario, Canada L3R 1B4
Penguin Books (NZ) Ltd, 182–190 Wairau Road, Auckland 10, New Zealand

Penguin Books Ltd, Registered Offices: Harmondsworth, Middlesex, England

First published 1989

Typeset in Times 11/13pt by
Goodfellow & Egan Ltd., Cambridge
Printed and bound in Great Britain by
Richard Clay Ltd., Bungay, Suffolk

A CIP catalogue for this book is available from the British Library.

ISBN 0 7207 1886 4

Contents

To Mum, for all the years she sadly never saw.

ACKNOWLEDGEMENT
I would like to thank Dad, Annette, Wayne and Darren
– the team that provided me with the motivation to
make all this possible.

1 Growing Up the Hard Way

LIFE HAS PROVIDED me with so much since those heady days in Sheffield, back in 1979, when I won the World Championship in my first year as a professional. Looking back on it now, I could never have foreseen how much of a difference it was to make, not just to me but the family as well. And what a contrast it has proved, particularly to those early days back in my home town of Llanelli.

The family has always been very important to me and one of the greatest pressures I have felt throughout my playing career has been the struggle not to sacrifice this one vital principle. I am sure I speak for most professional sportsmen and women when I say that success may bring financial rewards but often the price is a high one to pay.

Character plays a vital role not only in achieving this success but also coping with it when it comes. Unfortunately this is something that can and does take its toll on both family and friends. I am sure that my background and upbringing – at times sad and often quite turbulent – has stood me in good stead over the years.

As a child I remember life was never easy. I was the youngest of three children and until my mid-teens relied very heavily on sister Lynn and brother Barrie. Lynn in particular took on much of the responsibility of looking after the family, since my mother suffered from ulcerated legs and was often in considerable pain when she walked.

Although we were well looked after, money was always tight – as it was for a lot of people in our part of the world. My father was employed at the tin plate works in Dafen. The job was tough and poorly paid and he worked long hours to make up for this. Mother helped when she could with part-time jobs such as door-to-door

1

selling and some cleaning, but these were made more difficult with the leg trouble, which often incapacitated her.

Like all families, we had our ups and downs and a fair share of crises. But on the whole we stuck together in what was often a strained but nevertheless happy environment. Trips out and special occasions were few and far between. Even a visit to the cinema was a real treat. I used to get so excited I would run all the way to the bus stop and wait impatiently for my mother to catch me up, since she could only walk very slowly at the best of times.

One highlight of the year was the Sunday School outing to Tenby, which I really used to look forward to. That involved a two-hour bus ride – what a trip! Nowadays, of course, you just jump in a car and you're there in half-an-hour.

Other than that, we had to make our own entertainment. Most of the time we spent at Stradey Park, where we played soccer or cricket, or at Peoples Park. I remember once seeing a lad there with not only a bat and a ball but pads as well. I thought his family must be millionaires! In the summer I used to swim a lot and most days after school I would be down at the beach almost until it got dark. If I was not playing sport of one kind or another I would spend hours down by the railway line train-spotting. Occasionally I would borrow a friend's bike and cycle to Swansea to watch the trains there, which was quite an event.

Nowadays it is almost unheard of for children not to have their own bikes. For us, it was a question of borrowing what you could from those few friends lucky enough to have such luxuries.

It is hard to appreciate things like that now. But I am sure that because there was so much we had to do without when we were young we have since learnt the true value of money and possessions. It would be inconceivable in this day and age not to have chicken more than once a year, for example. But this was the family's treat at Christmas.

Of course as youngsters we did not really understand this. It is only when you look back that you realise how your standards of living have improved out of all recognition, particularly in my case with the success I have had playing snooker.

There were incidents that at the time meant nothing at all and only more recently have I been able to appreciate their real significance. For example, I recall having to go down to the local store for the shopping when mother was too poorly to go herself. I would take in the list of things we needed and the manager, a chap called Richards, would come up and tell me we could not have anything that week because we had not paid the last bill. I used to go back empty-handed and tell mother what had happened and thought nothing more about it.

How times have changed!

As I said, my sister was a big influence at home in those years before mother died. She did an enormous amount of work around the house and really looked after us all, even though she too was still at school.

As a child I was never very close to my father. This was probably because none of us saw very much of him. He was always working and when he was home we were out playing. It was not that he did not care for us, but because he had to work so hard he had very little free time at home in which we could do things together. Nonetheless he had a heart of gold. I recall sometimes sitting with him when he was eating his meal after work and he let me share his chips because he knew I was hungry. On the rare occasions he took us out, we would often walk to the reservoir at Swiss Valley, which was a couple of miles out of town.

Naturally I was a lot closer to my mother, because she was at home most of the time. Since her death, however, my father and I got to know each other a lot better and now, since he no longer works, we have become the very best of friends. Without doubt he is my number one fan and watches me play whenever he can.

Inevitably with an older brother, growing up was a tough experience. Barrie was not allowed out unless he took me with him, which pleased him no end, as you can imagine. So I was always mixing with boys that much older than myself, since he would have to drag me along when he went out with his friends. I was not only the youngest but also the smallest – hence my nickname at the time of 'Tich' – and had to take messages for them and always ran the gauntlet when we were doing something we shouldn't, like stealing apples. Guess who went over the fence to get them while the rest waited on the other side?

We quickly got the reputation of being a bunch of 'hellers', which I have to confess was quite justified, and parents in the area would warn their children off getting involved with us. In fact things got so

3

bad at one stage that if ever there was any trouble in the neighbourhood, the finger was always pointed at the Griffiths – much to our parents' dismay.

I suppose it was only a matter of time before we brushed with the law, although my brother and I did feel pretty aggrieved at the first incident. In those days we had very little in the way of toys and it was common practice to borrow from those who did. We had been playing with Nicholas Ward, who lived over the road. He had a huge collection of dinky toys which Barrie and I decided we would like to play with. So one morning, early, we sneaked over to the conservatory where they were kept and filled a small suitcase full of them to play with at home. Later that morning there was a knock at the door and mother, who went to answer it, was confronted by the local policeman. Meanwhile we had grabbed the suitcase, rushed out of the back door and chucked it over the wall at the back of the garden. But the toys were still scattered all over the parlour floor because we had no time to clear them up. Obviously we protested our innocence, but to no avail. We were accused of stealing. We knew there was something wrong, but it really did not seem that bad. Believe it or not, we were put on probation for that.

Clearly this was done as a warning, but what I could not understand was how one of my friends could take the attitude that we had been stealing. I could not accept that we had pinched the toys; we had just borrowed them. He had some and we did not. It therefore seemed to me quite reasonable that we should be allowed to enjoy them as well. I was nine then.

The next incident was more serious. I must have been about eleven at the time and one day Phil O'Shea and I broke into the rugby club's refreshment hut at Stradey Park, where we played every day. We were bored and just wanted to look and see what was in there. Phil was really my brother's friend and one of the hard boys in the gang. I remember feeling that I would do anything for him just to impress and be treated as an equal.

It was obviously a pretty foolhardy thing to do and made more ludicrous since there was no chance of finding anything in there anyway. But we broke off the lock and went in. As we were looking round for something to pinch we heard a noise and turned round quickly to find a policeman filling the doorway. He grabbed hold of Phil and led him off to the station at Pwll. I was so scared I just trailed behind, crying my eyes out. So there I was, back on probation.

There were plenty of other incidents during what was a wild and typically boyish period of my life. Some, I have to admit, were sheer acts of vandalism, such as when we used catapults to smash the street lamps. This made us very unpopular with the neighbours, who at one stage virtually ostracised the whole family. This really upset my mother. Needless to say, we again ended up in trouble with the law.

We were always on the scrounge for free drinks, which included a raid on the store room behind the local country club, now the Stradey Park Hotel. All we found there were a few bottles of mineral water. We had more success in someone's garage, which had rather carelessly been left open. Barrie and I took home what we thought was blackcurrant squash and hid the bottles in an old washing machine in our garden shed. It turned out to be home-made wine, which made us both horribly ill and earned us father's wrath into the bargain.

Unfortunately the local shops did not escape our attentions either. One favourite trick we used to play in the market was to throw our school caps on to the stalls and then pick them up with whatever they happened to land on. Sometimes this back-fired, such as when we snatched up a record – Apache by The Shadows. The problem was we did not have a record player at the time and it was at least six months before we finally heard the tune. We also used to pinch balls from Woolworth's since we could never afford to buy them. But because we were never very good liars we would often be found out. I used to kick around with Phil O'Shea's younger brother Tony, who was the same age as me. We were playing cricket in his back yard with a stolen ball when his mother came out and asked us where we had got it. Instead of telling her we had found it, to my horror Tony owned up straight away, which I did not think was a very smart thing to do.

Although we regarded incidents such as these as just harmless fun, one particular antic very nearly ended in tragedy.

The gang were messing about in the old lodge at Stradey Park. Prophetically my father had only the week before taken us past the derelict building, which incidentally my grandmother used to live in, and warned us of the danger of playing there. Brother Barrie was

5

clambering around inside when the chimney collapsed and fell on him. If it had not been for the prompt action of a lady called Mary Jenkins, who saw the accident and came over to help, Barrie would certainly have died. She tore up her petticoat and wrapped the pieces round his wounds to help stop the bleeding until the ambulance arrived. I recall seeing the ambulance take Barrie away. I was only eight at the time and did not appreciate the seriousness of the accident. I just knew they were taking him away and I missed him terribly. Barrie was in hospital for months and we were all desperately worried as to whether he was going to pull through. That certainly slowed us down for a while.

With such a dubious record of misbehaviour, one would hardly have expected us to be angels at home either and, particularly in the earlier years, my poor sister Lynn inevitably bore the brunt – being the only girl. I lost count of the tricks we played on her, which always ended up in a chase round the kitchen table. Fortunately she rarely caught us. One of Barrie's favourite pranks was to slip into the local fish and chip shop and loosen the tops of the salt and vinegar dispensers. We used to do this to Lynn at home with the tomato sauce, which invariably ended up all over the kitchen walls.

We would also put cockroaches in her boots and wait for them to crawl up her legs. One day she really lost her temper and on her way out – it was raining at the time – she launched her unbrella at us through the kitchen window. That window proved especially vulnerable. If it was not an umbrella, then it was a football or some similar projectile.

When I look back now, our parents must have been exceptionally tolerant, considering what they had to put up with. My father in particular had a very slow fuse, although it did ignite one Sunday dinner time. Barrie and I were playing in the front parlour when we were called in to eat. After half-an-hour we still had not turned up and, despite a thorough search of the house, no-one could find us. This was hardly surprising, since we had lifted some boards and crawled underneath the floor. The inevitable chase ended in the garden shed and for the only time I can remember father got out his belt to us. I can't say we did not deserve it.

School, I regret to say, was no different. I started off at Old Road Primary School, where I was always getting into trouble for something or other. Poor Lynn could not escape there either, since she was in the Junior School while I was attending the Infants. She would often be called in when a problem arose.

It is strange the little things you remember about schooldays. I recall quite vividly the problem I had with my shoes, which were too big for me. I used to love playing football in the playground, but had enormous difficulty keeping them on my feet when I was running.

We could not afford school dinners, so each lunchtime I would go home to eat. That was about a mile and a half away – and uphill. I used to run all the way there, bolt my meal and then tear back to school so that I could play a bit more football.

Because of what we got up to as a gang outside, my reputation followed me into school and for a while I was regarded as one of the tough boys. That was until one day I had a fight with my best friend Eric Watts, who incidentally went on to play rugby for Llanelli and later joined the professional ranks as a league player. He gave me one hell of a clout in the playground and that rather shattered my image among the other pupils.

Amazingly enough, with all the trouble I used to get into, I still found time to learn and was, by general standards, quite a bright student. Well, I did manage an unconditional pass into grammar school at the age of eleven, much to the delight of my parents.

I was really thrilled at the time, too, but probably more for the fact that my parents had promised me a bike if I passed the exams. The problem was that Barrie was then working as a paperboy and needed a bike for his work. He could not afford one himself and got my father to persuade me to lend mine. I was also doing a paper round each morning and I remember Barrie used to come and find me when it was time to go to work and take the bike off me. I had to finish my round on foot. He let it get into a terrible state and before long it was completely ruined. The annoying part about this was that he was being paid an allowance of £20 a month towards the cost of running a bike but always pocketed the money himself.

My parents' natural sense of pride at having a son in the grammar school soon turned to despair, however, when a year later I was expelled for constant mitching. (To any foreigner, that is playing truant.)

The real problem was that by now I felt very much one of the lads and all my friends were at secondary school. I thought the grammar school was too posh and felt horribly out of place there. Everyone seemed so much better off, which in turn gave me a feeling of inferiority. In short, I hated the place and eventually decided to stay away. In fact I managed to skip a whole term, although my parents never knew because they were usually out working at this time. When I could not go home, I would wander down to Stradey Park. Even if my mother was around, I knew that with her bad legs she would never come out and find me.

Eventually the school wrote to my parents and you can imagine the result. My father came down one day to the park and gave me a real hammering. He was furious – and rightly so. Back I went to school, but not for long. I just could not stand it there. I pretended everything was back to normal and as far as my parents were concerned it was. But I soon started skipping school again and I think I only attended one half-session in the whole of the next term. That was enough, as far as the school was concerned. I was expelled and told to attend the secondary in future.

I cannot explain how good I felt about this. I really believed I had finally made it – I had done something in my life. I was going back to where I belonged – to my friends – and I was going back a hero, the boy who was big enough to be expelled by the grammar school. Or so I thought.

Little did I know of the nasty shock that was awaiting me.

My first day at the secondary school arrived and I strode in feeling on top of the world. I was so cocky and did not even think of dressing up. I went in wearing jeans and a T-shirt. My new form teacher was Raymond Thomas, who now lives in my village outside Llanelli and who was for many years a good local cricketer. As I went and sat down at my desk, he came in, took one look at me and said, 'Hey you, Griffiths, out here.'

So I got up and swaggered down to his desk. As soon as I got within reach, he grabbed me by the ear, turned me round and said to the rest of the class, 'Look here, boys. This is Griffiths. He's just been thrown out of grammar school and I don't want you to have anything to do with him.'

Suddenly I was feeling terrible. This wasn't how I had planned it. Then he turned to me and said, 'What do you think of these clothes you've got on, then? Go home, change into your grammar school uniform and come straight back here. And be quick about it.'

I have never felt so humiliated in my life. Not only was I being shown up in front of the rest of the class and put in my place well and truly, but I also had to wear my old uniform. In a way, that was the worst of it, since the two schools had always been arch rivals and I was going to stand out like a sore thumb. But it was a marvellous thing for the teacher to do and just what I deserved.

Once I had had the chip knocked off my shoulder, I settled down and was very happy at school. My performance in class was not too bad either and I particularly enjoyed maths and English. Unfortunately it was the practical subjects, like woodwork and metalwork, that let me down. I never have been very good with my hands – except when they're holding a cue, that is.

Soon after I joined the secondary school, there was an incident that I mention only because it highlights the complete change in my overall attitude. I had scratched my leg on a rusty nail and did not bother to do anything about it. After a week or so it went sceptic and I was in agony. Lynn finally noticed something was wrong and was furious when she found out what had happened. I explained to her that I was frightened to tell anyone in case I was put off school. After mitching at the grammar, I thought I would be punished if I missed even a day. Lynn was marvellous. She took me off to hospital to get the leg treated and then went to the school to explain what had happened and get their guarantee that I would not be in trouble for it. In fact, I was off for a couple of weeks.

It was about this time that Lynn got married. I remember the wedding very well, if only for the fact that I got horribly drunk. Nothing unusual for a wedding, you might say. But I was only eleven at the time and it certainly taught me a lesson. I swore then that I would never drink again – and I haven't really, apart from the very occasional glass just to be sociable.

Sport was starting to figure very largely in my life. I got into the school rugby team, which was a great thrill for me. When I was picked – at full-back – I used to walk round the yard outside the school wearing the team colours and felt I was the king. It really was something special for me. We had a pretty impressive team, as it happened, which included several players who went on to gain international honours. They included Phil Bennett and Derek Quinnell and one or two, like Brian Butler, who later turned professional and went north to play league. We were unbeaten for three seasons and won every competition going. I was quite stocky

9

and lacked pace. But it did not matter in those days, because the full-back was primarily there just to stop the opposition. You never joined in the threequarter line. That was unheard of. If you did, you would not be picked again.

Remembering my own experiences, I can understand how important sport can be as part of school life for any youngster – and can appreciate what it has meant to my two sons – Wayne and Darren.

Although I was a lot more settled at secondary school, I suppose one has to accept that a leopard does not change his spots – at least not that quickly. I could not keep out of trouble totally and had my fair share of wackings. But, contrary to what has been written in the past about me, I did not do a lot of mitching at this stage, since the discipline was a lot stricter than at the grammar. Although later on I did sneak off during the lunch periods to go to the local snooker club Hatchers, I did not miss school to play. I was by now beginning to grow up mentally and took a more responsible attitude to life.

I can honestly say that the snooker bug only really hit me when I was fourteen. Up till then I had not been particularly interested, although we did have a small table at home which the family played on, especially at Christmas. That was mainly through the influence of my grandfather Freddie who many years before had been one of the best billiards players in Wales. My father used to cut down old standard length cues for us to play with and I remember commenting on this years later and being quite annoyed that he had ruined perfectly good cues in this way.

The more time I spent down at Hatchers, the more snooker got hold of me and it was not long before I wanted to do nothing else but get on the table and play. Now I was counting the days till I could leave school and have more time to myself – and, more especially, earn some money to pay for the table. At this stage I had no ambition to become a top player. I was just happy to knock the balls about. I had fallen in love with the game of snooker.

2 Getting the Bug

DURING MY LAST year or so at school, all I ever really wanted to do was get on a table and play snooker. Everything else seemed to be an unnecessary evil that just got in the way. I went to Hatchers snooker club in Llanelli, which was owned by Fred Hatcher, a very good local billiard player, and run by his two daughters, Dolly and Maisie. They were so good to me. Of course, at fourteen I was really too young to be playing in the club and would often spend hours just watching the others. But they would let me play on a table out of the way and this gave me tremendous encouragement.

It used to cost sixpence to play on a table for twenty minutes, which seems ridiculously cheap now but was a lot of money in those days, particularly for a lad who only had 2/6d pocket money a week. The family never had any spare money to give me, so I would save up everything I could just to play on the tables.

We had a system in the club where the loser paid for the table, which proved very good grounding for me. If I lost too often, I could not afford to play for the rest of the week, which used to break my heart. So I had to play hard – and learn quickly, otherwise I would not get a game. Sometimes Dolly or Maisie would let me pay on tick so I could stay on the table and I would pay them back the following week when I had some money.

I had a lot of fun at Hatchers in those days and owe an enormous amount to all the players who helped me there, particularly those team players who used to give me a game. Even Fred Hatcher himself would come over and watch me play and sometimes point out what I was doing wrong. Gwyn Roberts, who worked at the club, was another very good player and he also gave me a lot of help and advice.

11

I got a nickname in the club – it was either Snowy or Blondie, because of my very light hair – and I stood out like a sore thumb, particularly because I was so scruffy. But generally they did not seem to mind that. The first team were my idols then. Although they were not that old, they seemed so to me and I really looked up to them, hoping one day I could be as good.

When I ran out of money, which happened quite a lot to begin with, I would as I have said watch the others playing. One night I was in the club as usual when the captain Howard James came up to me and asked if I would like to play for the team that evening. I was overwhelmed and just stood there looking at him. My mind had gone blank. I could not believe my luck. When I eventually found my tongue, of course I said yes. I was put against a chap called Les Morris, from the Morfa club, on the first table in Hatchers. You can imagine the thrill that gave me. Incredibly I won the game 68–21. I will never forget the score, even that long ago. That was the biggest occasion of my life so far.

The following season I was allowed to register for the club, but because I was still officially too young to play in matches the captain had to get the other team's permission for me to compete. He also had a few words to say about my appearance. I was as usual pretty scruffy, but never gave it a thought until he came up to me one day and suggested that the least I could do was wear a tie for matches! But without doubt the most embarrassing moment for me came when I was playing in the club on a table that had just been re-covered. I went to take a shot and, to my horror, the cue caught the brand new cloth and ripped it. Fortunately everyone was very understanding, but I felt terrible about it.

For any snooker player, high breaks become a landmark. Before long I was scoring in the 40s but got stuck on 48 for quite a while. Then finally I broke the magical 50 barrier, shortly before I got into the club team. It then seemed to take an age for me to improve on that until one evening. I was practising before a match – against Llanesco – and made a 75. I felt on top of the world that night and everyone in the club was talking about it. What seemed then such a good break for a young player would probably go almost unnoticed these days, when even younger players than I was are making centuries every day.

The difference then was that without the television coverage snooker was not considered a major sport and you did not see so many kids playing it. So a break of that size for a lad of fourteen was regarded as something quite special.

When I came to play my match that night, against Ralph Edwards whom I got to know very well later on, I was full of confidence – too full, as it happened. We finished up with the game resting on the black. I missed the ball completely – a thin cut into the middle pocket – and lost the match. That proved a very important and timely lesson to me – that high breaks in practice do not count in matches and however well you are playing beforehand, it is what you do on the night that matters. Good practice form can lead to over-confidence which in turn leads to lack of concentration. Matchplay demands concentration on every shot.

I played for the club six times in my first season and finished up with three wins and three defeats, which was not a bad start for someone my age. But by the next season I had earned a regular place in the A team and was looking to win every match. The order of play was worked out on a handicap basis, and being the junior player I always went on last of the six. I went through the season losing just three or four games.

The following year, 1963, I tasted real success for the first time, winning the town's individual championship. My opponent in the final, at the Electric Club, was Winston Tegg, who had to give me 10 start a frame. I beat him 3–1. This was the biggest match of my life then and I remember practising beforehand on the small table we had at home. I used to imagine my opponent there with me and think all the time that I was playing against him. Looking back this may seem strange for such a small match. But of course at the time it was not a small match to me.

So there I was, having won my first championship and, at the ripe old age of sixteen, was the youngest player to have done so. The pride I felt then was only surpassed when, a couple of years ago, my eldest son Wayne also took the title and with it my record. For he was just a month younger. What a thrill it was – my son taking the record off his father.

During this period when I was playing local snooker I also entered what West Wales tournaments I could to get as much experience of competitive snooker as possible.

In the early days I started using another club in the town, the

Lucania, which was also run by two ladies, Gladys and Margaret. To begin with, I was happy to run errands for them and get cups of tea, all for a free game now and then. The highlight for me was when Gladys let me have a game on the number one table, which was a real honour because normally only team players were allowed to use it. Imagine, playing on the match table in the Lucania. I had not yet played any team snooker, but at fourteen I really felt like the king.

There was a great craze for gambling in the Lucania in those days and I used to spend many happy hours watching the older men play for money, though I never did myself. Inititally, of course, I never had enough to gamble with anyway, but even later I was never tempted. Some of the best players in the town would come into the club and I used to learn a lot from watching them. Not everyone can do this, but I used to get a great thrill from watching and still enjoy doing it now.

Many of the regular players in the club were out of work and used to go to the club after they had picked up their dole money and gamble it on a whole range of different games on the snooker tables, which sadly you rarely see played now. If you go into any club today, it is just snooker. In those days you could watch pool, lexicon, skittles, golf and other variations. Golf was a particularly skilful game, where you would play two-ball and work your way round all the pockets in turn or try to block your opponent from doing so.

I have very happy memories of the Lucania in those early days. Sadly it was later turned into a social club, although more recently it has reverted to snooker through a succession of owners – Mackworth's, Riley's and Midsummer Leisure. I myself recently looked at buying the club, although the deal finally fell through.

I shall never forget the people in the Lucania, particularly Con Harris. He was an inveterate gambler – on horses, snooker, anything that gave him a chance to win money. I used to love watching him play. I can also remember him and Margaret, who helped run the club. They were engaged at the time and were always quarrelling. She would then send him messages, the contents of which I never saw but could certainly guess at.

Although I did not get involved in the gambling, I played a lot of 'loser pays' in the club and, as my snooker improved, did very well at it. Typical of a young player, I would try to pot everything. Safety was non-existent in my game; I just did not know of any other way to play.

Hatchers, however, will always be my favourite because it was where it all started. I can see the club now, up on the second floor, with its seven tables in a straight line down the room. As you came in from the stairs there was a tiny bar area where you could get soft drinks and light refreshments. Sadly it is no longer. When the lease ran out the club closed. Incredibly at that time they could not get rid of the tables. I remember a stonemason took away all the slate beds and the rest they threw away. What a waste that was, when you think how much tables cost today.

It was during this time, in the autumn of 1962, that I left school and took my first job in the colliery at Graig Merthyr. I had to start in the Cae-Duke training centre, after which apprentices were sent to whichever colliery had vacancies. The reason I chose this was that the money for someone my age was so much better. I believe I earned £4 or £5 a week, whereas in other trades it was as little as 30 shillings. When you consider that my father would have been earning about £14 in the tin plate works, this was big money for a youngster.

Working in the mines was a great experience for me. Not only was it my first job, but I was in a totally male-orientated environment with people much older than myself. It was certainly tough and you learnt to grow up very quickly.

It was quite a life. I was up each morning at five and had to catch a bus (even at that time of the morning!) to Pontardulais, where the train was waiting to take us up into the valley. I would arrive at the colliery in time to start work at seven. It was a long hard day, then I would leave off work to catch the train and then the bus, which would get me home about four in the afternoon.

I was not used to heavy labour and what with the early mornings and the tiring work in the colliery I would come home absolutely exhausted. But it was tremendously valuable experience. I had my own job, money in my pocket and I was learning a lot from the men I was with.

I was put in the blacksmith's shop under a marvellous character called Sid Gwenter. He was a real expert at his job and, in fact, has recently made the gates for my new house. Goodness knows why they put me there, because I was useless with my hands and would

15

never make a blacksmith as long as I lived. I could manage a bit of welding, but that was about it.

Sid was very kind to me and I learnt a lot from him in other ways about life in general. He was the one who took me for my first ride in a car, which in those days was something special. I shall never forget it was a fawn Morris Oxford with a column change. He even let me have a go driving it. What a thrill that was.

Sid also tried to correct my bad behaviour, such as swearing which like everyone in the colliery I used to do a lot. He did not approve and one day dipped me in the 'bosh'. That was the water they used to quench the hot iron. 'If I ever catch you swearing again, Terry,' he warned me, 'I'll put you right in.' Needless to say I did and Sid was as good as his word. It's funny how you get out of a habit, but it was a long time before I swore again.

I worked for a while on the surface and also had some training on the coal face itself. Because Sid was also the fire-fighting officer at the colliery, we had to make periodic visits to all parts of the mine and were therefore two of the few people who had ever seen every district there. Most of the miners only ever worked on their own coal face. That in itself was an experience I shall never forget.

We used to go down late in the morning and would take a ride in the empty drams that were being sent back to the face to be refilled with coal. Graig Merthyr was a drift mine and there were no shafts to use to get to the face. Those rides, in the drams, were sometimes quite terrifying. They used to fly along the tracks when they were empty and often jumped off the rails and crashed into the sides. I remember the winders saying to me, 'Go on, don't worry. You'll be alright.' I used to think it was all very well for them. What if they were in the drams and not me?

When we had inspected down below, we would come back up on the loaded ones, unless we waited until the end of the shift. This was just as dangerous since, sitting on top of a pile of coal there was virtually no headroom. If they came off the rails, we would have been decapitated. But despite all this, it was very exciting.

One of the most extraordinary experiences at the colliery was taking a shower for the first time. I recall vividly going into this long shower room and glancing down the line at all the naked miners and thinking, 'Good God, look at all the different sizes they've got!' After a week or so I got used to the idea and took no notice. I did, however, have a lot of trouble with my mop of blonde hair, which used to go a very funny colour with all the coal dust. I could wash it three or four times, but it did not seem to make any difference. In the end I had it all shaved off. It was only then that I realised what a funny shaped head I had – like an egg at the back, it was!

A few of the boys from my school also worked at Graig Merthyr, but I found myself making friends with a lot of the older workers. It is difficult to explain to anyone who has not experienced working in a mine, but the comradeship was fantastic. And I can tell you that to lose a workmate was devastating for everyone. Although the safety in mines is a lot better today, there used to be quite a few accidents and it took weeks of going back to the colliery before you could get something like that out of your mind. Fortunately I never saw anyone killed, but just to know it had happened and share the grief was bad enough.

When I was sixteen, I bought my very first means of transport – a Lambretta scooter, for which I paid the princely sum of £20. That was followed by a blue Honda 125. That was great and I used it to get to work. What a luxury! It meant I could leave for the colliery an hour later. My only real mishap on it was a ticket I picked up for speeding. I was caught one morning on the way to work doing 50 mph down a steep hill. I felt particularly hard done by since it was only six in the morning and there was nothing else about – except the police.

I spent a couple of good years at the colliery, by which time I had begun to realise that although I probably had a job for life if I wanted it, there was not a lot for me there. I was also tempted away by extra money. My brother had recently got a job on the buses and was earning £11 a week. The chance seemed too good to be missed and so I became a bus conductor.

Apart from having a clean job for a change, the thought of mixing with the public also appealed to me. And I have to confess that the one thing that really turned me on was the uniform. That was the business, I thought. I even had a crease sewn down the front of the trousers to keep them looking tidy. As a lad of seventeen, dressed up in uniform and standing on the open platform of my own bus, I felt ten feet tall.

I had continued playing snooker while I was working at the colliery, but I was pretty tired by the end of an evening. And there

17

was always the thought of having to get up early in the morning. With the bus job the hours were slightly more sociable and I took advantage of this to play more. I was now playing snooker at the YMCA in Llanelli and for a while virtually lived there when I was not working. In fact my father remarked one morning when he saw me that I seemed to be spending too much time there. He had seen my motorbike outside the club on his way to work in the afternoon and it was still there when he came back at two in the morning. Around that time I started competing in the West Wales League, which provided me with a much stiffer challenge and enabled me to achieve the next milestone in my career – the West Wales singles title.

My opponent in the final was Jim Selby of Neath, a far better player than me at the time. In fact Jim and I played each other a lot in those days and were later both selected to play our first international for Wales against Ireland in Dublin. Since then Jim has become a very good friend and now runs the Star snooker club in Neath.

It was particularly important for me to win this final since it was being staged in front of my own supporters in the Llanelli Conservative Club. I had not started well and in the first frame found myself 26 points adrift with just the green and the rest of the colours to go. Somehow I managed to snatch that frame with the help of a snooker and went on to win 4–0.

To this day I am convinced that had I lost the frame I would have been the one to lose 4–0 since the occasion was a very heavy one for me and Jim was the better player. But the effect of that first frame was to boost my confidence and knock Jim's back. So there I was, West Wales champion at seventeen and suddenly I realised I had something to offer. I knew perfectly well that there were probably at least forty players in the league who were better than me on paper, but now I was the champion.

I had further successes in this championship, but that victory without doubt was the most important and proved to me that I could play against the best (in the area, at least) and win. My game was certainly starting to move in the right direction and the following season I recorded my highest break to date in a league match. That was 90 and you can imagine how thrilled I was, particularly since that turned out to be the highest championship break of the season as well.

3 Settling Down

UP TILL NOW my life had revolved around work and snooker and I had thought little about other teenage pursuits, such as girlfriends. To be honest, there was never much time for anything else. But as I settled into my new job on the buses and had established myself as one of the better local players, my thoughts did turn in that direction.

I had passed my driving test at the first attempt and bought an old Mini. Naturally I was terribly proud of it until, just a few weeks later, the thing all new drivers pray will never happen did. I was coming back from the YMCA one evening and drove into Island Place, when I saw this car coming towards me on the wrong side of the road. I tried to avoid him, but with so little experience I really did not have a chance. He hit me broadside – and in full view of a policeman, who had been watching the whole incident. Worse was to follow since I had been insured with Fire Auto Marine, the company that went bust. What a start to my driving career! Fortunately my sister Lynn was able to get the necessary parts at cost and I managed to get the Mini repaired. But that hurt my pride – and my pocket.

I found having a car very useful, since I and my friends would drive round town looking for girls to pick up. Usually we would take them to the beach. It was a lot of fun, but never got too serious. Then I went out with a girl call Ruth Dickson, who worked in the delicatessen. It was while I was with her that I met Annette, who also worked in the shop. She was already courting, but eventually I persuaded her to come out with me. In fact I remember chatting her up on the bus one evening. I was working the late shift and she happened to get on my bus. She stayed on for several stops while I worked my charm. It obviously did the trick, because shortly afterwards she finished with her boyfriend and went out with me.

We did what I suppose most courting couples do, meeting up whenever we could after work and going dancing and to concerts at the Glen Ballroom, which I was later to turn into my own snooker club. When the weather was fine, we often took my sister and her family out in the car for a picnic. On one occasion we found this delightful spot out on the Gower with a really lush stretch of grass. So we settled down and spread out the picnic. We saw people walking in the distance, but thought nothing of it until a ball flew perilously close and we suddenly realised that we had parked ourselves on a golf course. We very soon had the picnic repacked and beat a hasty retreat to the car.

Holidays had been a rarity when we were children, so I was reasonably enthusiastic when it was suggested we all went off to Barmouth camping. Annette came with us. To say our hopes were dampened would be an understatement. Almost from the moment we got there it poured with rain as only it can in West Wales and that put me off holidays for a very long time – and camping for ever.

We did manage a laugh or two while we were there, however, particularly when we decided to take a boat out on the lake at Butlins. We were going quite nicely and had rowed right out to the middle when we lost an oar. Annette started to panic as the boat went round and round in circles. As she shouted to the rest of the family on the bank for help, people started gathering until there was a great crowd all round the lake, laughing their heads off.

Eventually we got back, much to Annette's relief. The joke did not end there, however. It was at the time when Francis Chichester was sailing round the world in Gypsy Moth and later that evening I mentioned what fun it would be to sail round the world too. Of course, that set everyone off again, because if I could not handle a rowing boat on the lake, how was I going to handle a sailing boat on the ocean. And for the rest of the holiday we only had to mention Gypsy Moth and we all got the giggles.

Ironically Annette was never very interested in snooker, although she never seriously tried to stop me playing. I must admit there have been times over the years when she would have liked me to, but she has really been very good about it. However I was beginning to realise that there was more to life than going to the club every night and, when we decided to get married, I actually gave up playing for a while. My father was not at all pleased, but I wanted to see as much of Annette as I could and at the time I was working lots of double shifts to earn as much money as possible.

I finally put the question when we were shopping in Swansea one day. We had gone in to get some clothes and Annette was reluctant to chose a ring because she did not know how much I could afford. On the way home we stopped at Kidweli to celebrate with an ice cream and then went home to tell the family.

We had agreed to save £5 each a week, three of which we each put into this car I had bought on HP. It was a yellow 1100. As Annette reminded me afterwards, it was just as well we did get married, otherwise she would have lost half that car! Saving was made a little easier by the fact that I had changed jobs again. A friend of mine had got me into the Post Office, where I was now earning £14. With overtime I could bring home a good £20 a week. To keep costs down, we later agreed to sell the car and I bought a Honda 250, which was the 'in' bike at the time.

When I went to collect the Honda, from Eddie Stephens in Camarthen, I had great difficulty getting it going because it was a left-hand foot change. On the way home, I felt I had won the pools flying along on this beautiful red and white bike. Then it came on to rain. I could not stand the thought of getting this brand new machine wet and so I stopped at the next bus shelter and took it inside until the rain stopped.

Over the years I have had more cars and bikes than I care to mention. I love driving and the sensation of speed, although I have never been a reckless driver. Motorbikes, in particular, can be very dangerous in the wrong hands. But the thrill of opening up the throttle was something I have never lost. Even now, I would love to have a selection of bikes in the garage and it is only because Annette is terrified of them that I have not.

My pride and joy was an FJ 1100 Yamaha, which cost £3500 and was very much the bike at the time. I bought that in 1983. I had not been on a motorbike for thirteen years and I recall a friend of mine, Mike Stride, offering me a ride on the back of his. I had almost forgotten what a great feeling it was. That did it. I made up my mind to get a bike again and went for the best there was.

I shall never forget Barry Hearn's reaction when I asked him for a cheque to pay for it. Barry, of course, became my manager in 1982 and looked after all my financial affairs as well as the snooker. He said: 'Don't be silly, Griff. Keep taking the sensible tablets.' Annette was totally against it, of course, but I had made up my mind.

I had the bike for about eighteen months and really enjoyed it, especially in the summer. But every time I took it out, Annette nearly had a heart attack, so eventually I gave in and sold it.

Our wedding was a fairly quiet family affair. We were married at All Saints Church in Llanelli on January 25th 1969. What made the day extra special was the fact that my sister Lynn had persuaded mother to come. I was the only one of us three she actually saw married. Previously she had refused because of her legs, as she thought everyone would be looking at her. Lynn had got some special bandages which did not look too obvious. We had our reception afterwards in the Gardenia Restaurant. The only real disaster that day was with the pictures. A friend of my father, who fancied himself as an amateur photographer, insisted on taking all the official pictures. Not only was there chaos round the church, but none came out. So the only record we have are a few family photos that relatives took.

Annette and I had a short honeymoon at her grandfather's place in Kent. I shall never forget the first time I saw Bert. He had come to Llanelli to meet me and was staying at the Stepney Hotel. When he invited us to dinner one evening, Annette went into a panic because I had nothing smart to wear. I used to live in trousers and sweaters and did not have a suit or jacket to my name. My brother Barrie offered me one of his, but I looked terrible in it and Annette flatly refused to let me wear it, much to my relief. So I turned up as I was.

To get to Bert's house we had to travel through London, which for me was like flying to the moon. I was twenty-one and in all those years had never been out of Wales. When we got to Paddington, we took a taxi across London to catch the next train from Charing Cross. Well, I just froze for the whole ride. God alive, I had never experienced anything like it before and I was terrified. It is incredible now, looking back on it. I have flown all round the world since then, but I was so naive and had led a very sheltered life up to that point. I think Cardiff was probably the largest place I had ever been to before. We both laugh about it now, but at the time it was horrific.

We were on honeymoon for a week and the only problem we had was when we woke up each morning. Bert would insist on bringing us up a cup of tea. Neither of us could stand the stuff then, although I drink gallons of it now, and as soon as he was out of the way I used to run downstairs and tip it out in the toilet.

We had arranged to live with Annette's parents, Tom and Audrey, until we could save up enough money to get our own place. They are a great couple and I thoroughly enjoyed the two years we were with them. Because we were all at work during the day and I was often out playing snooker in the evening, we really only saw each other at weekends and so there was little time for us to fall out. The only occasion I really upset them was when I had the Honda. I used to keep it in the garden shed and would ride it over the lawn. It was not long before I had made a muddy track all over the grass, much to Tom's disgust.

But what Annette and I really wanted was our own home and this we finally got in September 1970, just two months before our first son Wayne was born. It was a little two-bedroomed house in Island Place, right in the centre of town, just up the road from where Lynn now lives with her family and my father. There is no chance of getting a blue plaque on the door now; they knocked the place down some years ago and it is now a car park!

We paid £1500 for the house, which seemed like a fortune to us at the time. But somehow we managed. Although Annette's parents had been very good to us, it was great to have a place of our own.

Hardly had we settled in when I became a father. The day Wayne was born I had come off the morning shift and rang up the hospital from the phone box on the corner to see if Annette was alright. She had already gone into hospital. I then went to bed, only to be woken later that afternoon by my sister to tell me I now had a son. Of course, it was a great thrill, but I do not think I fully appreciated it at the time. I was too young and had not experienced enough of life to take it in properly.

Annette was quite annoyed when I turned up at the hospital, not only because I did not get there earlier but also because I had not brought a present. Fortunately for me, it was early closing in the town, so I got away with that by the skin of my teeth. I was not so lucky a few weeks later, when mother and son were back at home. A mouse had been discovered in the kitchen and I had strict instructions to get rid of it by the following morning. Unfortunately I forgot and rushed off as usual on my morning shift.

Since Annette was awake too, she decided to go down to the kitchen and do some ironing. As luck would have it the mouse decided to make an appearance as well. This was too much for Annette, who ran out of the kitchen screaming and shut herself upstairs with Wayne until I came back off shift, refusing to go anywhere near the kitchen till the mouse was taken care of.

Having Wayne to look after meant that Annette had to give up her job. She was working at Morris Motors and earning good money. Although she later organised some part-time work in the evenings, life again became very difficult, particularly with the mortgage to pay as well. I did as much overtime at the post office as I could and was still trying to fit in my snooker.

The pressure inevitably began to tell. Annette had her hands full at home and I was either out working most of the day or playing snooker in the evenings. Although she tried to understand, I knew she hated it really. She would expect me to be home by a certain time and then got annoyed when I arrived back late because a match had overrun. We never went out together and I could see she was starting to resent my playing. This had been happening over a period and we had many an argument about it.

Although this situation did not improve when Wayne was born – or when we had Darren two years later – I am sure looking back that they did indirectly help to cement our marriage at a time when we might easily have split up. And there is no doubt that had that happened, it would have been the snooker that was to blame.

At least I was a little more in favour when Darren was born. This time I actually made it to the hospital and was not lying asleep at home. I remember going back to get some snooker books to read while I awaited the birth. Although Annette was not particularly keen on the subject matter, she was prepared to excuse me one weakness on this occasion.

Poor Annette really wanted some life outside the home and I never gave her any because when I was not working I was always out playing. I owe an awful lot to her tolerance during this period because, although I again gave up playing locally for a short time, she knew that all I really wanted to do was play snooker. Had we known then what was to happen to our lives later, it might have been easier to accept. As it was, we both went through a very rough time.

That period had not been made any easier by my mother's death a few months before Wayne was born. She had been suffering for many years, as I have already said, but that did not make us any more prepared when the day came.

Looking back, I never felt I treated my mother well, although as a youngster I suppose I was like any other son. She was having increasing problems with her legs, which had to be dressed every day, and being short and a bit overweight did not help. In the later years she hardly left the house, not just because it was so very painful to walk but also because she was very self-conscious about the bandages on her legs.

She was seeing the doctor more and more and on the occasions she went into hospital she told us she was just in for a rest. On the last occasion I went in to see her, assuming it was another of her 'rests', I walked straight past her bed. That was a terrible experience. My own mother was lying there and I had not recognised her. The hair looked a lot greyer and she had lost so much weight. After I talked to her for a while I felt happier and left thinking no more about it.

The next thing I knew was that the hospital had rung my father to tell him she would have to have one of her legs amputated because gangrene had set in. When I heard this, I remember thinking that I did not want her to have a leg off because I knew how much she had suffered over the years and the struggle she had had to come to terms with the bandages. To have her leg off now would be the finish for her. Then they told us she would have to have the other leg off as well and within 48 hours the gangrene had spread into the rest of her body.

After all that time, suddenly it had come . . . just like that. If she had been in a road accident, perhaps I would have felt differently. But it had gone on so long through her life and now . . . I remember Annette commenting on how cold I was towards my mother's death. The problem was that for a while I just could not accept it. I did think to myself that it was the best thing that could have happened, because having both legs off would have been terrible. I think if I

25

had been living at home at the time, it would have hit me a lot harder.

Later on I used to get periods of thinking how badly I had treated her and how much more I could have done for her. This hit me most when we had our own children and I started to realise what family life was all about, bringing up children. I often felt . . . I suppose guilt is the wrong word . . . it was more than guilt. And it has gone on throughout my life. One of the worst things about it was that she never saw Wayne or Darren.

My father moved in with Lynn and suddenly part of my life had been taken away. Now I was married and starting my own family and I had a whole new life of my own to lead. My success in snooker brought it all back to me. I know I have made a lot of mistakes in my life and had many regrets. But by far my greatest regret has been that my mother never saw me become a father – or world champion. And it was only after her death that I realised how much it would have meant to her. When Lynn was clearing out her things, she found a handbag with all the newspaper cuttings about me and my snooker exploits. Until then, nobody knew they were there.

Of course it is great that my father has been here and seen me succeed. But we were just an ordinary family and for her to have seen her son do so well . . . I know now how much she would have appreciated it. I have achieved everything in my lifetime since she died and that really sums it up. It is not only the snooker. There is the family and my life at home, especially now the way things have turned out with the new house and the club.

I may not have cried a lot when my mother died, but I have shed many tears since. At the time it hit my father and Lynn worst. I remember little of the funeral and much of what happened immediately afterwards is still a blurr. But gradually over the years of being a parent it has come home to me more and more. I think that is why I am now so close to my father. My snooker has brought us closer together because he loves the game so much and travels around with me whenever he can.

4 First Taste of Success

IN JANUARY 1971 I was laid off work through the national postal strike, which lasted about thirteen weeks I seem to recall. I was practising a lot then, since basically I had nothing else to do, and was playing much more snooker. It was during this period that I scored my first century break. I did a 130 clearance on 21 January 1971 – how can I ever forget the day – against another postman John Lloyd, a very good friend of mine. We had played together in several teams over the years.

Of course, that was in the YMCA and I thought it was a particularly nice gesture on the club's part to have a special plaque made and fitted to the table. In fact, it is still there to this day.

It's strange how, when you reach a special milestone like that, you often repeat it very soon afterwards. The following week I got another century and later that year achieved my third. All of a sudden I felt a definite surge forward in my standard of play.

The first century had proved quite a barrier for me. I had come so close to it so many times. The nearest I had got before was actually in a match, when I missed the black on 93 against Billy Williams from Garnant. It was a difficult black which I had to play using the long rest. I missed it and went in off. I had already done a 90 break in the tournament, but just could not get through the 100 barrier. I had lots of chances, but my nerves just kept getting the better of me and I failed.

There was one thing I remember about the 130 break more than anything else – apart from the fact that I was thrilled to have done it, because it was the highlight of my career so far. I went running up through the town centre to get home to tell Annette because I was so excited. When I got to our house in Island Place, I burst through the door waving my arms in the air and said, 'You'll never guess what's happened. I've just got 130.' Annette could not understand what I was on about until I explained. Then she really put me down by saying, 'Oh God, I thought we had won some money or something.'

I will always remember that because she really put it into perspective. It did not mean that much to anyone else – and why should it? But for me it was fabulous to score my first century, because it gave me a lot of confidence. It also made me stop and think: I can play this game; I'm better than I thought.

Shortly after the strike was over I changed jobs yet again and was now an agent with Pearl Insurance. I joined the company again for a lot more money. And, of course, the prospects for an insurance man were a lot better than for a postman.

I had worked for the post office for three years and there it was all about seniority. That was the big thing. The longer you had been there, the better the round you were given. And I recall a lot of the older postmen, who had been there all their working life and never even considered that there might be other jobs in the world, saying to me, 'Can't understand you leaving, Terry. You'll lose all your seniority, you know, if you ever want to start back here again.' And I always reflect back on that. It was advice given in the best spirit, but very narrow-minded. They thought the postman's job was the one you should stay with all your life. I suppose I could have worked my way up through the post office, if I had stayed for another twenty-five years.

Really, though, being a postman had been an enjoyable job, meeting the public all the time. I was delivering in the van as well as sorting the mail. And looking back on it – working on the buses and being an insurance agent – those jobs certainly helped me when I went professional, because I was so used to mixing with people.

The pay at the post office had not been bad and did go up quite a bit when I was there. We also got a fair amount of overtime, which helped. But it was a hard, tiring job again involving early mornings all the time. I seemed to have spent all the early part of my life getting up early in the morning and I always felt tired by the end of the day.

I used to work as much overtime at the post office as I could. What with a young family and the mortgage to pay on Island Place, we were always short of money. They were long hours. I would be out walking the streets delivering mail in the morning and then standing around in the afternoon sorting. All except Wednesday, that was, because then I had a match in the evening and would try to swop shifts with someone that afternoon. And I would even run round with the second delivery so I could get more time at the YMCA club practising.

I remember having a nickname at the post office; 'Ding Dong' they all used to call me – after my time as a bus conductor. There was a good spirit there, particularly at Christmas, when the atmosphere was something special. There was, of course, a lot more work and we had extra temporary help in, which was fun.

I also played a fair amount of cricket for the post office and really enjoyed it. Len Jones, one of the leading players at the YMCA club, was in the team and we had a reasonable amount of success. I usually kept wicket, but generally enjoyed everything – batting and fielding.

I did like my job as a postman, I must be honest. In fact, I enjoyed all my jobs at the time. But I wanted to get on.

When I moved to the Pearl, I think I went from something like £18 a week at the post office to being an insurance agent that guaranteed about £40 a week, with more if I did well selling policies. So it was a big move. And it was the first job that did not involve me in getting up at the crack of dawn every day. For nearly ten years I had had to go to work early – first in the colliery, then on the buses and latterly with the post office – and it was crucifying me.

There was a good friend of mine, a chemist called Geoff Tucker, who used to get to work at 9.30 every morning. I used to think he was God. Just imagine what it must have been like to go to work at 9.30! That's how much it meant to me. I used to look forward so much to my rest days at the post office, because I could have a lie-in – not a day off, because I enjoyed the job – but a lie-in. That's how much it meant.

Getting that job with the Pearl was a very good move. I loved book-work, probably because maths had been my favourite subject at school – and there was a lot of it, I can tell you. Another advantage was that I knew plenty of people in Llanelli, having lived there all my life and through my links with snooker, so I had a lot of leads for selling insurance which certainly helped me in the early days. Also I have always found it easy to get on with people, which again helped with that type of job. It is like when I turned professional; being able to mix and talk with others is a great asset.

From the family's point of view, my new job enabled Annette to go back to work, since I would make most of my calls in the evening when people were at home. During the day I would do the paperwork, look after the boys and, of course, get some valuable practice in on the snooker table. Annette's contribution during this period was tremendous. Often when she got home from work, she would give a hand with the bookwork in the evening while I was out making calls.

Although I was never an ideal father when Wayne and Darren were still babies, I really loved looking after them as they grew up. Annette was off to work early each morning so I would get them their breakfast. I used to make them porridge and I remember on the first few occasions putting the pan outside on the shed roof to cool down. I soon had to stop this habit, since the cat suddenly took a liking to the porridge as well and used to help itself when I was not looking. The first time this happened, Annette came home and asked the boys if they had enjoyed their porridge. Wayne shook his head. 'We never got any today. The cat ate it.'

I grew to be quite domesticated, too. Because Annette had so little time to do the household chores, I would often wash the clothes and hang them out to dry. I did, however, draw the line at ironing. And I would always have the tea ready when she came home from work.

On the whole, the boys were very good and I really enjoyed being with them. To begin with, however, there were a few scares with Darren, who was then not yet three. One of the problems was that he had found a way of getting up on to the window sill, opening the window and climbing on to the roof of the shed outside. Fortunately an observant neighbour rushed in one morning and warned me of the pending disaster. Despite repeated attempts to thwart this dangerous habit, he persisted and in the end we had to fit locks on to the window so he could not get out.

Although with my insurance job and Annette's, money was a lot easier than it had been, there were times when we did get very stretched. I remember during the miner's strike my insurance business dropped off badly and I took a temporary job driving taxis in the evenings to keep some money coming in. But we survived and, most importantly for me, I grew very close to both the boys.

Snooker was now playing more and more of an important part in my life and I decided to enter the Welsh Championship for the first time – that was in 1972. I suppose it was mainly because of my three century breaks and the fact that I felt I had made the vital breakthrough. I knew hardly any of the top players in Wales. Of course I had heard of them but had rarely seen any of them play. So I was really taking the plunge into the unknown. I must admit I was very fortunate that year with the draw. The big names kept getting knocked out before I had to meet them – top amateurs like Alwyn Lloyd, Terry Parsons and Des May.

So there I was at the semi-final stage, where I had to play Dilwyn John, an international who also played soccer for Wales. In fact Dilwyn was quite an all-round sportsman. Anyway, he was a better player than I was, but I still beat him 4–2 and that put me in the final against Geoff Thomas from Ferndale. I got to know Geoff very well after that, although at the time he was only a name to me – and a very big name in Welsh snooker.

Everybody was telling me, 'You'll beat Geoff easily.' So of course by the time I went into the final, as far as I was concerned, I had won. Incidentally, the winner of the Welsh Amateur Championship automatically went on to the World Amateur Championship, which that year was due to be staged in Ceylon. For someone who had only been as far as London – and that just once – the thought of a trip to Ceylon was the end of the world. And I remember going round telling all the people I was collecting insurance money off, 'I'm going to Ceylon next year.' I was only in the final, you know, but by now everyone had convinced me that I would beat Geoff easily.

Now Geoff has had a marvellous amateur career since the early Sixties. He got into the 1974 final of the World Amateur Championship and is still playing to a high standard now. Although he never looked particularly good, he has always been a very hard match player – very efficient. I remember watching him in a match with Scotland against David Sneddon, who is now a professional player. I had been watching this frame and glanced up at the scoreboard. Geoff was 40-odd points up and I thought to myself: They've made a mistake with the scores. Watching the game it seemed as though he had not scored anything. They had not, of course. Geoff had quietly compiled several breaks – and that was very much his style. I have often thought back on that; it was a real object lesson for me.

Anyway, I played Geoff in the final. By the interval I was 4–0 down and my world was collapsing around me. I remember going into the mid-session break. Sandwiches had been laid on but I was not hungry. Nobody spoke to me and I did not know anyone there to talk to. None of the officials came up to me – or the players – and I felt so lost. I think that was definitely the lowest point of my career to date.

I went back out and won the first two games and almost took the next. I felt I was getting back into the match and it really gave me a lot of confidence in myself, because I knew I was at a very low ebb. I had performed well under extreme pressure at that level and that cheered me up a bit. I should have made it 4–3, but instead lost the next frame and that was it. The match finished 6–2. On reflection, however, I had no complaints. Geoff had been a far better match player.

What came out of that final, which hurt me most, were two things that, in my opinion, changed my career. One involved the Welsh selectors. Leading to the final, everyone had said to me, 'You'll be in the Welsh team, now.' But after the final the chairman of the selectors, Mal Hendra, came up to me and said, 'We're giving you a game as a reserve for Wales this year to give you some experience.' That was a crushing blow, because yet again I had listened to other people and they had all said, 'As you're runner-up, you're bound to be in the Welsh team.' But it served as a very important lesson in life – not to listen to other people's opinions all the time.

But the one thing about that final, more than anything else, was for the first time in my career I had accepted defeat. Mario Berni from Neath, one of Wales' best amateur players, whom I had great respect for as a player and who became a very good friend, had told me a few years before, 'Until you accept defeat, you'll never get on as a snooker player.' But until then I could not understand what he meant. At the time I had thought: Accept defeat? Good God, what's he talking about. I hate losing. But when it happened against Geoff Thomas in the biggest match of my career – the final of the Welsh Championship – and I was well beaten, I always remember going up on to the stage in Abercwmboi, where we played, for the presentation. I said a few words and thought to myself: I've accepted that defeat within myself. Anyone can put on a brave face and smile; there are loads of them in the professional game. But there are not many good losers as such.

There is an interesting point here about accepting defeat. When you have given your best with every shot and played with total concentration, then it is a lot easier to accept that you have lost. The opposite situation is where you have gone in with a carefree attitude of: If I win, I win; if I don't, I don't really mind. And although they may seem miles apart, mentally there is a very fine dividing line between the two. It is amazing how close you can be to taking one attitude or the other and what a difference it can make to the effect of defeat when you wake up the next morning. It is easy enough to look back and say the other guy was lucky and excuse yourself by the fact that you were not trying very hard. But that type of defeat is a lot harder to accept later on.

I always believe every player gets chances to win. If you miss those chances, then you only have yourself to blame. It is no good making excuses, such as the run of the balls. Again it was Mario Berni who put this in a nutshell. When you have two balls on the table, they will never move until you hit them. They are just sitting there – completely static. So whose fault is it when they do not run correctly? Certainly not the balls, since they cannot move without you playing them – and it is the way you play them that affects how they run.

When I look back, that day changed my whole outlook on winning and losing at snooker. I did not think so at the time, but it definitely was the moment when my attitude changed. It was the first time I had got good vibes from another player's skills. Because I could appreciate how well Geoff had played, I was able to accept that defeat. And thank God I can still do that now. From that day on, my career went forward and I think that was one of the main reasons for it.

Anyway, I was not selected to represent Wales and I did not go to Ceylon. Ironically nobody went. As it turned out, Ceylon backed out of staging the World Championship and, believe it or not, Wales played host instead. Being the home nation, we could now put four players in to make up the numbers – and I thought I now had a good chance of getting in. But they still did not select me. I was very disappointed, but it made me realise that possibly because I was from West Wales, I had to win to be selected for these things. All the selectors were from East Wales and, to be fair to them, they had seen all their players but never really seen me.

I was determined my chance would come, although unfortunately the following year in the Welsh Championship I went out in the early stages of the competition. But I now started to set my sights a bit higher. I had tasted some success against the best players and, once I had got rid of the disappointment of losing that final in 1972, I appreciated that possibly I was still too inexperienced.

Then came two matches that made all the difference to me. One was against John Prosser, a very good amateur at the time, who hammered me 4–0. The other was against Elwyn Richards. Incidentally both men played down at my club recently. Elwyn is still a very dangerous player and on that occasion also beat me 4–0. It was the first time I had seen these two. Of course I had heard about them, but now I was playing

33

against them. They both performed very well and the 4–0 scoreline was certainly a fair result in both cases.

I came away from these two matches thinking: If they're the best players in Wales, I know I can win. They hammered me on the night because they both played well. But I looked at them and thought: They haven't done anything on that table that I can't do. That gave me a tremendous boost of confidence, more so than getting into the 1972 final of the Welsh Championship probably. Those two hammerings set me up and I made up my mind to put in a big effort in the Welsh snooker scene at top level.

Although my ambitions to achieve full selection to the national side had so far been thwarted, I was being chosen as a reserve. The first occasion was at the Cosmo Club in the Rhondda, where Wales were playing Ireland. The tradition was that the reserves from the two teams opened the match by playing the first frame. So of course I was all keyed up and wanted to play well to boost my chances of a full place in the team. I was matched with Paddy Thornton and getting ready to play when, to my amazement, a woman stepped forward. Apparently, as a courtesy, the wife of the Irish Association's chairman, Gloria Ruanne, had been invited to get the match officially underway by breaking off. I just could not believe it.

The following year, 1973, I was again picked as a reserve for Wales, this time against England at Leeds, an event that proved memorable for me purely because of an hilarious incident while we were staying up there. The first night we were there, we got back to where we were staying rather late. It was getting on for midnight and I was starving hungry. So Mario Berni, who was of course our captain, said he would try and get them to rustle something up. He found a waitress and asked if we could have some sandwiches and a large pot of tea. 'Certainly, Mr Berni, I'll see what I can do.'

Sure enough there soon arrived two of the largest plates of sandwiches I have ever set eyes on and a huge pot of tea. Mario turned to me and said: 'Who's going to pay for all this, Terry? It's certainly going to cost a bit.' Anyway, we all tucked in and thoroughly enjoyed it. After we had finished, the waitress came back in.

'Did you enjoy that, Mr Berni?'

'Yes, thank you, it was lovely. In fact, do you think there's any chance we could have the same tomorrow night as well?'

'Certainly,' she said, 'but do you think you could do me a favour, too?'

'What's that?' replied Mario.

'When you next speak to your relatives, would you ask them if I could have some more money?'

There was a pause. Then suddenly it dawned on us. The place we were staying at was a Berni Inn! And she thought Mario was one of the family.

There is another little incident that Mario often reminds me of which involved myself and John Prosser, the man who had given me that hammering not so long back. We were up in Llay playing a representative match against North Wales and had gone up the night before and booked into an hotel. The following morning Mario got out of bed and drew his curtains. As he was looking out of the window he saw what must have been to any observer one of the most comical sights ever. It was barely dawn and there were John and I, dressed to kill with our dickie bows and flaming red Welsh waistcoats, walking off down a country road clutching our cues and looking for somewhere to practise. There's keen for you!

And I was very keen at this time. I was determined to make the national side and so I started entering a lot of competitions. I went into the Welsh area of the English Amateur Championship, which involved a lot of travelling by car. I also played in invitation tournaments all over the country – London, Grimsby, Middlesbrough and Warrington. In a way, I was now becoming a semi-professional snooker player. Of course I was still working and had my family to look after. So there was not a lot of money about. When I look back on it, I do not know how I managed it financially. We never had any money to spare. You used to get some expenses, but they nowhere near covered what you were spending. When you consider that I might go to Middlesbrough five or six times perhaps just to win £100, then even if I did win the tournament I was still well out of pocket.

The English Championship was the one you needed to get into and to do so you had to qualify through the Welsh section first, which without doubt was the hardest to win. Once you had qualified through that, you had a fair chance in the English. This is divided into Southern and Northern areas and from Wales you go into the

Southern competition. At this stage there are sixteen players left in each section and the winners meet in the all-England final. But to get out of Wales was the hardest task.

To win through you had to beat four or five of the top Welsh players, of whom probably at least three were better than me. It was like being in the last four of the Welsh Championship. Then of course you had to get through the Southern section, which was in fact a lot easier. Even still, there were some good players around, people like John Virgo, Ray Edmonds, Patsy Fagan, Willie Thorne and, yes, Steve Davis as well. All these are now professionals, too. But there were a lot of other weaker players. In Wales, they were all strong.

I first qualified for the English Championship in 1974. That was a big step forward to me, winning the Welsh area and getting into the Southern section of the competition. This involved travelling to Chelmsford, where I was due to play Vic Harris. That meant a long, long drive from Llanelli in an old Escort I had at the time. I had only just bought the car and because the wheels were not properly balanced it shook when you drove it over 40 mph. It was also the time of the petrol shortage and the speed limit was down to 50 mph.

Mario Berni kindly volunteered to come with me as driver and I remember having to warn him that the car had a very fierce clutch. Poor Mario! He had only just got his driving licence and did not understand what I meant until he got in to drive and found out for himself.

After a very tiring journey, which involved crawling through London as well, we finally arrived ten minutes before the match was due to start, having left Wales at seven that morning – nearly eight hours before. Needless to say, I was hardly in the best shape to play a crucial match like this and before I knew it I was 2–0 down. Although I staged a remarkable recovery to lead 3–2, the effort was too much and Vic won the last two frames.

I had lost my very first English Championship match and the journey home seemed even longer than before!

I learnt another very good lesson that day. I shall never forget Mario's words afterwards. 'Terry,' he said, 'whatever the result, you must leave every venue in such a way that they will always have you back.' I hope over the years I have lived up to that very important piece of advice.

In the meantime I had finally got into the national team, having been selected as a reserve for a couple of seasons. I made the national team for the last two matches of the 1973/74 season. My first full international was against Ireland in Dublin, and I played Pascal Burke, who is now a professional too. It was a terrifying experience and I left it pretty late – finally winning 2–1 on the black ball. Then we played Scotland in Edinburgh, where I beat John Phillips 3–0. I was delighted. My first taste of international snooker and I was unbeaten after two matches.

My first international in Ireland was a tremendous experience for me. And according to Mario Berni, it marked the transition from being a potter to becoming a player. But as much as the victory that was so important, since I wanted to make a good impression, I remember particularly the clinics Mario used to hold in the hotel ballroom. We would all sit round in a circle and have a question and answer session, with Mario as the chairman. It was great fun.

Beating Pascal in my first-ever international holds special memories and brought about a relationship that has continued over the years. He was with Doug and myself on the trip to the World Amateur Championship in South Africa and I remember his wife Helen, who went with him, looking after our washing while we were there.

And Pascal was one of the first players to come to my club when it opened a couple of years ago. He mentioned then that he wanted to buy a snooker club in Pembroke Dock and I told him that if he did I would be happy to come and open it for him. Sure enough, he did – at the beginning of this year – and Annette and I went down for the opening.

On the way to the club she asked me what fee I was getting. 'None,' I replied. 'You mean to say you are doing a show for nothing?' I explained that the story went back a long way and I had agreed to open the club for him. That was that. At the end of the evening Pascal, a typical Irishman, could not thank me enough and presented us with the most magnificent cut-glass decanter. I was overwhelmed and thanked him profusely, adding that it was totally unnecessary. Afterwards, Annette said: 'Now I know why you did the show for nothing.' And that is right. That special evening had brought back a lot of memories for me – not least my very first international for Wales all those years ago.

That year, 1974, turned out to be a very significant one for me, because in September I had my first taste of playing in front of the cameras in the HTV South Wales Echo tournament in Cardiff. It proved to be a great success because I won it, beating an old adversary

Dilwyn John in the final. But the match I remember best was the semi-final, where I played Mario Berni.

I was 42 points down with one red left and I snookered Mario. He missed the shot to give me a free ball and I cleared the table. The blue and pink I potted were probably the two easiest shots I will ever have to play in my whole career. But I went down for each one thinking: I'm never going to pot this ball. It was the pressure of the television cameras and lights that got to me – something I was lucky to experience early on and which now I do not even think about.

They were very easy shots and I got them both, leaving myself a very difficult black. Curiously I felt no pressure with that shot at all and potted it, putting myself in the final. These matches were one-frame affairs and therefore very nerve-wracking. Fortunately the final was the best of three.

It had been an excellent experience for me at that stage to win on television, to suffer the nerves and the tension on easy shots. In all, I played in this tournament for four years, winning it twice and losing in the final once. And the exposure it gave me was also important. The tournament was on television a lot, because they used to show one match a week on Sports Arena, the local sports programme.

Playing on television had another very significant effect on my life. Because the tournament was pre-recorded, I had the chance to sit back afterwards and watch it. And when I saw myself on television for the first time, I was horrified. I was so fat. At that time I weighed fifteen and a half stones. I was so embarrassed I virtually stopped eating for a week or two and managed to shed a total of three and a half stones over the next three months. That got me down to twelve stones, which I have stayed at ever since.

5 Spreading My Wings

WITHOUT DOUBT, the most enjoyable period of my career so far was between 1971 and 1977, when I was playing as an amateur. Even with all the success I have had since, the professional game does not come anywhere near to it. Reflecting back now, I certainly got the most fun out of the game in those years.

And that really highlights the difference between amateur and professional and the way in which money can spoil the game. You see, all of a sudden I had ambitions and aims in the game that I had never experienced before. Now I was starting to win at all levels, but for every rung of the ladder I went up, there were another ten to climb. It just keeps you going all the time.

Of course there was all that travelling to do – seven and eight hour journeys in some cases. And at the end of it I had some good wins and I had some thrashings. But for the first time it took me out of my home environment and, through doing that, when I became professional I was used to playing away all the time. I was also very used to having to travel before I played a match.

These days, I know, players are travelling all the time, week in, week out. But in those days there were very few fellow amateurs who had even played out of Wales, maybe through lack of transport or finance or possibly ambition. So I was one of the few Welshmen to spread my wings – Doug Mountjoy was another who was doing it.

Interestingly enough, out of that period we were the only two Welshmen who turned professional. But I suppose that shows what effect it had on us, travelling round and taking on the best players in the country – often in their own home towns. I got hammered quite a lot in those early days, which is something you have to learn to swallow. But it was all very good grounding for me as a youngster.

At that time my main Welsh rivals on the table were Terry Parsons, Geoff Thomas, John Prosser, Alwyn Lloyd, Des May, Roy Oriel, Mario Berni, Doug of course and John Terry, who was more local. They were all top quality players – internationals. And because none of them had probably heard of me, let alone played me, I was always the underdog.

Looking back, if any of them were apprehensive about playing me it was probably because of that – not because of how good or bad I was, but because they did not know me or how I played. I was a fresh face on the circuit and they did not know what to expect. But for me, because all these players were big names, every game was like a final and I played in that frame of mind all the time.

From their point of view, too, they were under pressure since it would not look good for them if they lost to me. At least that was the situation in the early Seventies. But by the time I won the Welsh Championship in 1975, all that had changed. Winning the national title was definitely a very important breakthrough for me. Now, all of a sudden, I was a recognised player.

I had a very good season leading up to winning that championship and in the final, of course, I beat Geoff Thomas, the man who had beaten me in 1972. I was 7–5 behind and won the last three frames, which in itself was a great achievement. But what I recall most vividly about that final was my form. For three or four weeks leading up to that final, it had been really bad and I thought: I've had it. I'm not going to win this final.

Again it was a lesson learnt that form leading up to a big tournament (at that time they were few and far between) did not mean a thing. Your body reacts to the build-up and often you cannot put effort and concentration into your game beforehand. I think that is one of the problems in the professional game today. There is a big match nearly every week and it is difficult to build yourself up for each one. On the amateur circuit you had plenty of time to do that.

Despite my feelings at the time and the fact that I was trailing 7–5, I did pull back to 7–7 and went on to win. During the match Geoff had to go to the toilet and was away for what seemed to me like an age, although it could only have been a few minutes. I thought to myself at the time: It's obvious what he's doing this for – to settle himself as much as anything, but possibly to unsettle me as well.

Being the new boy in the final, all these thoughts were going through my mind. Geoff, of course, was used to this sort of occasion, having reached a number of finals himself.

I will always remember that last frame. I was thinking: He's not going to win this one. I don't care what happens, I'm going to win – and I did.

The excitement of winning the Welsh title was a great feeling and filled me with pride. But, as often happens on such occasions, I do not think the impact of it all really sunk in till later. And certainly there were moments when it all came back, such as an appearance I made shortly afterwards in Cardiff. That evening, as I went on to play, it was the first time I had been announced as the reigning Welsh champion. Standing there in my full evening dress and hearing those words was something very special.

But just as I was enjoying the sweet smell of success, I also had to suffer the rather unpleasant taste of acrimony. And sadly the cause was one of my early day heroes on the table, Alex Higgins. I am now talking about 1975, when Alex had taken the snooker world by storm. He was phenomenal, playing shots nobody had ever seen before. He was everybody's favourite, but he also had his bad image which unfortunately he has kept up even to this day.

The incident occurred when I put on a show for him at the Drill Hall in Llanelli. I had organised the whole event myself, sold tickets and got sponsorship for it. There were 400 seats in the hall and every one was taken. I even played as well, but really the important thing was that I had got a sponsor for snooker in Llanelli for the first time – that was the Felinfoel Brewery. On the night I caught an out-of-form Higgins and beat him. I did not play well, but Alex was bad. If he had played well, he would have beaten me easily.

The problem is that when Alex has a bad night on the table, his behaviour off it is worse than normal. After the show, he turned to the referee in front of everybody, the mayor and all the local dignitaries, and gave him a 'V' sign. I was disgusted. Then we went upstairs to the sponsors room, where I had arranged drinks for the local guests and, of course, Alex. My family were there, too, and I remember Alex kept putting his arm round my sister-in-law. My brother Barrie, who had had a few drinks, said, 'What's happening here?' Alex immediately turned round and took a swing at him. Barrie ducked and Alex connected with my friend Peter Francis.

41

All of a sudden a ruck developed and I was panicking. There were all these people I wanted to impress and now snooker was getting a hammering. Alex picked up a bottle from the table and said, 'Come on then.' Now I could see it was my brother-in-law's turn. John's temper was rising and he can be quite a handful when he wants to be. I took one look at his face and thought: That's it. I've got to do something now. So I ran straight at Alex to break it up, although I will freely admit that I was very frightened.

The whole night was now ruined – for me and for snooker sponsorship in Llanelli. I was very disappointed. Up till then everything had run well. We had had a full house and everyone enjoyed themselves. But Alex spoilt it right at the end.

The next day he was playing at another club up the road in Pontardulais and I had been picked to play him a frame. I walked into the club and saw Alex reading the newspaper – the horse-racing section, of course. He glanced up briefly – Alex never looks at you – and he just could not face me. To him I was a nobody and that disgusted me. He could have stood up and said, 'Sorry about last night, Terry. I got carried away.' It would have been forgotten, because I then idolised the player. But from that day on, although he has always had my respect on the table, he never had it off the table.

When the new season started the following autumn, I was really looking forward to proving why I was the current Welsh champion. This should have been my greatest moment. As it turned out, it was a disaster. My cue went and I kept losing to people while I tried to break in a new one. I had a terrible time finding one to suit me. The problem was that I had extended my original cue by adding a piece to the bottom. But the wood kept crumbling and in the end I just had to change it. It's at times like this that you really appreciate how important the cue is to a player.

There was, however, a positive side to all this. Fortunately I have always found in my playing career that defeats can, in an odd sort of way, help you. That season I was finding life very difficult. I was lacking in confidence because the cue problem was affecting my results. I was coming up against players I knew I had to play well against to beat and of course I was continually losing to them. If only I had my old cue again, I kept on thinking, I could beat them. Of course that was impossible and I had to find a solution. It was therefore a very valuable experience for me in my career – to accept defeat in the circumstances – and I came through it. It did take a while, however, for me to adjust.

Despite the frustrations I was going through with my new cue, overall I was fairly happy with the way my snooker was developing and I decided it was time I tried to make some money out of the game. After all, it had so far cost what to me was a fortune, but this was the first time I had even thought about getting something back for all my effort. Also I thought my recent exposure on HTV would help me get bookings. My idea was to go round and challenge club teams of eight and offer them an aggregate handicap of 250 points. If I won, I would take £15 and nothing if I lost.

I got a lot of help with this from Cyril Richards, who was then managing director of Billiards & Snooker Wales, a local snooker table manufacturer. Of course, Cyril had a list of all the clubs in the area and he helped me a lot with fixing up bookings. I got some letters printed and sent them out to the clubs, offering them an evening's challenge match. Money was still very tight, so the chance of earning £15 a night was a great incentive for me.

Having written to a club, I would then follow the letter with a phone call. More often than not the response would be, 'Who?' I would tell them, 'Terry Griffiths. I was on television recently.' Back would come the reply. 'Oh yes. You won that, did you? Okay, we'll put it to the committee.' I got quite a few matches arranged that way and it certainly eased the financial situation. And it was the first time I had actually earned some money out of snooker.

As far as the competitive scene was concerned, I again qualified for the Southern Area of the English Championship and was drawn to play Patsy Fagan in Acton. Patsy had reached the final the year before and was a hot favourite to win through again. Despite this and the tremendous support he got on the night, I beat him 4–1. My success was short-lived, however, since I was knocked out by Willie Thorne in the semi-final.

On the strength of my victory over Patsy, his manager Georgie Jackson invited me back to Acton to play in a Champion of Champions tournament, which involved myself from Wales, Patsy from Ireland, Eddie Sinclair from Scotland and Ray Edmunds from England.

Mentioning Eddie reminds me of a very amusing incident that

happened before the tournament began. Eddie had rung me on his way down to London to find out where I was staying. When I told him, he asked me to book him in as well. Some hours later he rang again and said he had not been able to find my hotel, but had managed to book in to another one.

'Where are you staying, then?' I asked him.

'It's a place called the Savoy!'

'Then for Christ's sake ask them how much they're charging,' I shouted down the phone. Even for someone like myself who knew little about London, the name alone had started the alarm bells ringing. Eddie went away to check and came rushing back.

'It's £100 a night. Where the hell are you? I'm not staying here.' So I had to drive over and collect him and he ended up sleeping on the floor in my room.

Now any match at Fishers, where we played, was always a great gambling occasion and before the tournament, while I was practising on one of the tables, a bookie came up to me. 'Are you going to be trying tonight, Terry?' he asked. I could not believe what he was saying and at the time did not understand what was going on. Typically of me, I replied, 'No, of course I won't be trying. I've just driven 300 miles to have a knockabout!'

It just shows you how naive I was at the time. It was only afterwards that I realised why he had asked me that. People were laying a lot of money on the matches and he wanted to know what odds to lay on me. I was quickly beginning to realise what a hard world snooker was becoming at this level in the game.

The following year, 1976, I again qualified for the Southern Area of the English Championship at the expense of Doug Mountjoy and was due to meet Geoff Foulds. After the disappointments of the last two years, I naturally wanted to do better this time and so it was important for me that I was in the right frame of mind for the match.

But as I have discovered many times in my life, mishaps have a curious habit of occurring when you least want them to. And so it was to be on the journey up from Llanelli. We had set off in an old Austin Allegro I was running at the time. My father and Peter Francis, who was a close friend and travelled virtually everywhere to matches with me during this period, were also in the car.

We were turning off the M4 into Brentford when the car broke down. The head gasket had gone. I can see it now. The three of us were standing round the car when the AA turned up. When the chap went to take off one of the spark plugs, a jet of water shot six feet up into the air. So I left the others to sort things out and made my own way to Acton.

Geoff Foulds was a very sound and steady player, very experienced too, and not the sort of person you would want to be drawn into a long match with. But the game was very tight all the way through and at 3–3 it was anyone's. The final frame went to the black ball, which Geoff potted. That was a terrible disappointment to me. Having worked so hard to get to this stage again, I had fallen at the first hurdle – and the incident with the car had not helped. I remember thinking: I've had enough of all this. That's the last time I play in the English. Of course, it was not, but that's how I felt at the time.

The situation was not helped by the fact that I was due to play for Llanelli in the Welsh Inter-Town Championship the following evening in Cardiff. Because the car was being repaired, I had to stay the night in London and catch a train the next day to Cardiff. When I rang Annette to explain I was not coming home, she was very annoyed and we had a big row on the phone.

The real reason for my defeat, however, rests I am convinced in an incident with Geoff a few weeks earlier. I had been up in Fishers again playing a challenge match against Patsy Fagan. Watching the match was Geoff Foulds. After the game a crowd of us around the table were discussing the draw for the English Southern Area, which I had not yet seen. Someone said to me, 'You're playing Geoff Foulds, Terry.' Immediately I replied, 'Who am I playing after that?' It was a harmless remark as far as I was concerned and I thought no more about it. But Geoff, who was right behind me, heard what I had said.

It was only a few years later, when I had got to know Geoff quite well, that he reminded me of that evening.

'Do you remember when you heard the draw and said "Who am I playing next?" You just took me for granted.' I suddenly realised what I had done.

'No, Geoff,' I said, 'I would never do that. I just meant who would I be playing if I got through.'

'Well, it didn't sound like that. And I'll tell you something now. That night I went home and I practised every day because I was so determined to beat you.'

It is funny how things happen that you know nothing about. But

45

Geoff came to that match even more determined than ever. It was a big match for him, too, but I had inadvertently given him that extra incentive – something I have always tried to avoid in my career. I would never say things like that to people. It is just not my nature, for a start. But it happened then without my realising it. And Geoff won.

I can look back on that match and make the problems of breaking down the excuse for losing. But I probably lost that game because of Geoff's determination to win after what I had said. Fortunately we laugh about it now.

It took me a while to get over the disappointment of losing to Geoff in the English but it did make me even more determined to make amends the following year – if I qualified. In the meantime I was playing a lot more amateur tournaments, which of course involved plenty of travelling around the country.

One venue I remember well was the Cyclist Club in Grimsby – so called because of the old bike that hung outside the entrance. For me it involved a round trip of about 700 miles and I used to drive up first thing in the morning, play my match, stop for a quick Chinese meal or some fish and chips and then drive straight back to be ready for work the next morning. When I tell you that the average prize money would be in the region of £80 or £90, then you can imagine what a costly exercise this was, particularly if I won and had to go back for the next round. But it was all valuable experience.

Another venue in the same area that I visited a lot was the Louth Town and Country Club. And it was on one of these trips I decided to take Annette and I rang round to find a good hotel we could stay at. We arrived at this particular place – a big hotel, it was – but for some reason there was no heating. So I went out and wandered round Louth looking for a cheap fire we could use in our room to keep warm.

Without doubt the real highlight for me in 1976 was the trip to South Africa, where Doug Mountjoy and I were representing Wales in the World Amateur Championship. Unfortunately, for one reason or another, it did not quite live up to expectations. I had already been selected on the strength of my Welsh title win against Geoff Thomas the year before, which bearing in mind my lack of success since was just as well. Doug joined me as the 1976 national winner.

Of course, we were both over the moon at the chance of competing for the world title, but the trip to South Africa was going to be costly and we needed some money for our expenses. So we agreed to do some shows together round the clubs. We charged £40 a night between us and managed about twenty bookings. That was a great help and I shall always be grateful for the support of those Welsh clubs for giving us a financial hand.

Believe it or not, this was the first time I had ever been abroad – and I was now twenty-nine. So my first experience of life outside Britain was to play in the World Amateur Championship, which was by far and away the biggest tournament I could compete in. That in itself would have been too much for me. But also I was going away for three weeks, the longest period I had ever spent outside Llanelli.

You can imagine what it was like for two lads from the Valleys. Doug and I arrived in Johannesburg and on to this vast luxury five-star hotel – The President. Until then, I had only seen such places in films. We walked into the lobby, which was bigger than anything I had ever seen in my life – apart from the hotel itself. It was all too much.

Doug and I booked in and went up to our room, which we were sharing. I remember going into the toilet and saying, 'Good God, there's a shower in here.' By this time my eyes were agog. I looked out of the window and saw the swimming pool. I could not believe it. It was as though we had just been let loose into the outside world for the first time. It was a fabulous experience – and totally overwhelming.

For the first two weeks we played on a round robin basis to see who qualified for the final rounds. Both Doug and I got through and now I had to play Roy Andrewartha. We tied our match and had to play again. I won 4–0 and so went on to the quarter-final stage.

Doug was a hot favourite. He had previously packed in work and was playing better than anyone. But a lot of people considered my chances, too. I was the quiet one coming through the other half of the draw – and I had also beaten Doug a number of times back at home. I knew I could beat him this time, because I had a lot of confidence in myself now. Then, all of a sudden, home sickness hit me like a sledge-hammer. It was the first time I had experienced it quite like this and I felt terrible. I could not sleep. I was not eating. I just wanted to be home. In the meantime, I had to play Jimmy van

Rensberg in the quarter-final of the World Championship and I just could not handle it.

Strangely enough, I was not the only one in a bad way. Before Doug and I left for South Africa, our wives had flown out to Spain for a holiday. Doug had won it in a competition and we agreed that since we were going to be abroad for three weeks we would let the wives take the prize. Doug had driven them down to the airport and Annette told me later how upset both she and Yvonne had been. While they were waiting for their plane, they just sat in the cafe crying!

I had promised Annette that I would ring her in Spain from Johannesburg. I could not get through so I sent a telegram, telling her to ring me at my hotel. Apparently when they received the message Yvonne panicked. As I had not mentioned Doug, she thought something had happened to him. To make matters worse, Annette had forgotten the time difference and when she phoned we were both out playing snooker. Eventually I got through and explained that Doug was fine. I was feeling wretched, of course, and continued phoning Annette after she got back home. I even wrote to her in Spain – the only letter I have ever sent Annette – and she never received it!

We had not really seen or experienced anything of the political side of life in South Africa, since we were either playing snooker or staying in the hotel. But one incident in particular left a very unpleasant taste in my mouth. We were in the lift with a South African couple when one of the hotel staff, who was black, tried to get in as well. The South African shouted some abuse and refused to let him in. I had never experienced anything like that before and felt pretty sick about it.

But my greatest problems now were on the table itself. I played Jimmy van Rensberg and lost 5–3. I had gone – that was all there was to it. And even if I had beaten him, I am sure I would have lost in the next round, because I was getting worse and worse. Being away from home in this strange environment full of gloss and money, I just could not cope. The last week of the championship was the longest of my life. I had to stay there because of my ticket, although I did try to change it, and of course I was there to support Doug. He was by far the best player in the tournament and won the final easily.

The South African trip had been a nightmare for me, when it could have been the scene of my greatest triumph so far. And, of course, I had gone out with every hope of winning the world title. On the day Jimmy played better than me and deserved to win. I would not want to make my home sickness an excuse for losing. But I knew that I just could not handle the situation anymore. I had beaten myself and let myself down.

Of course, I could not wait to get home and was mightily relieved when our plane touched down at Heathrow, where Annette and Yvonne met us. During the ride home we stopped off at the Memburey Service Station on the M4 for some fish and chips. And, without doubt, that was one of the best meals I have ever eaten. A little later, as we crossed the Severn Bridge, I remember seeing the 'Welcome to Wales' sign and feeling a great sense of pride in having been to South Africa to represent my country. Suddenly all the problems of the trip were behind me and all I wanted to do was come home next time as the World Amateur Champion. Of course, as events proved, that was not to be.

When I got back, all I felt like doing was to sit at home with Annette and the family. For the first few days we hardly left each other's side. We did not even watch television, which we would normally have done, but spent every hour possible talking to each other. It had been a very strange experience, but one that I am sure opened our eyes to a lot of things that had gone on previously in our life and threw us much closer together.

The other effect it had on me was to provide a fresh outlook on snooker. All of a sudden, I had ambition again. Prior to my selection for the World Championships, I had seriously considered packing in the competitive side of my game and just playing local snooker. Now all I wanted to do was win the world title. I had had my first taste of it and, despite the traumatic experience of being away from home, I thought I was good enough to win it. More than anything else I wanted to get back there. But to do that I had to win the Welsh Amateur Championship again, which would be as tough as ever. I did, of course, go on to win the English Championships, but that did not qualify me – only the Welsh national title could do that.

Ironically, I never did achieve that ambition. Although I did not know it at the time, I was to make a far more significant decision a couple of years later that was to change my whole life.

6 The Final Proof

IF 1976 HAD been the year of frustration on the snooker table, then 1977 was definitely one of fulfilment. I again qualified for the English Amateur Championship and this time made no mistake. After three attempts, I was determined to win that title. Having beaten Clive Everton in the Southern Area final at Acton, I was confident this was going to be my year at last.

Mind you, there was a brief moment of doubt when, just four days before I was due to meet Sid Hood from Grimsby in the final at Romford, I woke up with lumbago and could not get out of bed. After all the other hiccups of previous years, I just could not believe my luck. Surely I was not going to be frustrated yet again. With two days to go, I felt terribly depressed. I could only stand half upright and was suffering a lot of discomfort playing.

As a last resort, I went to see the physiotherapist at Trostre Steelworks in the hope that he could do something to ease my back. He manipulated it with his thumb and suddenly I felt something move. By the following morning I was feeling more or less all right. Mind you, with the back trouble it meant I had not played for nearly a week and all I got on the practice table when I arrived at Romford was about half-an-hour. Unbelievably, when the match got under-way, I hardly missed a ball and beat Sid 13–3 with a session to spare. It was a tremendous feeling. At last I was the English champion.

That final in the Romford Matchroom was significant for another reason, as things turned out, because it was also my first meeting with Barry Hearn, who later became my manager, and of course Steve Davis. I shall always remember how helpful Barry was at the time, giving me directions over the phone on how to get there and welcoming me to the club. And because the match was over so early, Barry then suggested I played Steve in an exhibition game for which he put up £50. I told Steve that I would only play if the money were split. Typically of Steve, he said he would have to ask Barry first! Anyway, we played, I won and we shared the money.

It is ironic, looking back now at that first meeting with Steve on the table. Although I did not know it at the time, our careers were to run together and he was to cost me millions of pounds, which is true really. If there is one single reason why I have lost a fortune in snooker, it would be Steve Davis, without a doubt. Throughout my professional career Steve has been there – all the time. To say he has been an influence on my snooker life would be the understatement of the year. He has dominated my career since I turned professional in 1978.

Typically Barry, who was never one to miss an opportunity for a party, had arranged a celebration at Ladbroke's after the match and generously invited us all to join in – including the lads from Wales who had come up to support me. That certainly completed a wonderful evening for me.

By winning the English Championship, I was now in a position where I could apply for professional status, because that was one of the ways you could qualify. And being the type of person I was, with a good reputation in the game, I was almost certain to have been accepted. But I held back. At that particular time I was not ready to make such a momentous decision. There was a lot to consider, not least the financial implications of relying entirely on my snooker to provide a living. Even in 1977 snooker was not what it is today. There were few tournaments and not a lot of money to be won. So unless you were the best, like Ray Reardon, you would not be guaranteed that good an income.

I remember Clive Everton spoke to me in Acton, when I had beaten him with probably the best snooker I ever played as an amateur. 'You'll have to think about turning professional, Terry, because the game is definitely going to become bigger in the next five years.' I thought: What is he talking about? I did not understand. The professional game was always big to me. I just could not grasp what he meant. But what he said then was so true, as events have since proved.

After the English triumph, the snooker magazines reported that my long potting was as good as any professional player. And I thought: Good God, is it? Things like that started to give me definite thoughts of turning professional, although I did delay a decision until after I won the English again the following year.

In the meantime I was getting a lot of useful experience in smaller events and was now considered the top amateur player in the country. Inevitably the question of becoming a professional kept nagging away in my mind and Annette and I discussed it over and over. But I must admit I was frightened of it. I had a good job in insurance, which allowed me enough time off to travel around and play in all these tournaments. And by now I was starting to earn a bit of money from snooker – not a lot, but some. I was not losing money any more, put it like that.

Immediately, however, my mind was diverted away from such thoughts by the fact that I had another very important match to play against Steve Newbury in the quarter final of the Welsh Championship. That was just three days after my English win and I was feeling great. I went in with loads of confidence and Steve proceeded to beat me easily 4–0. I could not pot a ball. At the time I could not understand why. Now I know. After the English Championship, this match seemed like an anti-climax – and Steve was too good a player to take on under those circumstances. I was shattered and remember driving back with Peter Francis and pulling into a layby, where I just broke down.

That defeat meant that for at least another year or two I could not go on to the World Championship. It was a bitter disappointment and again cast doubt in my mind about turning professional, since I really wanted to play in the World Championship again. But looking at it realistically, I was coming up for thirty and might have to wait a couple of years for another chance. What if I did not win the Welsh title next time? So all of a sudden I felt there was a lot of pressure now going into the Welsh Championship just because of this.

In the end, all these considerations finally helped me make up my mind to go for professional status and get out of the amateur game. But that decision was still some months away.

A few weeks after the English triumph and then my hasty exit from the Welsh, I went to Prestatyn to compete in the Pontins Open, which was then really the only Pro-Am tournament of the season. Every player who was any good used to go. It was a great gathering, the one week of snooker where the rest of the world wanted to prove they could beat the professionals. There used to be about 1000 entries, which were gradually whittled down to 24. They would be joined then by the eight professionals who had played in the Pot Black tournament to make up the last 32. The amateurs were given a 25 start per frame.

To qualify at Prestatyn was a way of earning money, because then you could pick up about £200, which was a lot of money in those days. But it was also the one time the amateurs had a chance to play the professionals off handicap. They could never play them otherwise in a tournament – not the top ones.

I had been to Pontins the previous year, but this time I was feeling pretty confident – and having qualified was looking forward to the tournament proper. It was tough going, because as luck would have it I played a professional in every round – Cliff Thorburn, Eddie Charlton, Perrie Mans and then Dennis Taylor. So now I was in the final and had to face Alex Higgins.

There were a lot of problems for Alex that year. For disciplinary reasons he had not been invited to play in the Pot Black competition. He had turned up for the series, but did not go to rehearsals and so they left him out. In those days, Pot Black was *the* tournament. If you were not in that, you were not in anything. Of course Alex was now such a big name it did not matter too much to him. But the snooker press gave it a hammering. How could you have Pot Black without The Hurricane?

Alex was determined to go to Pontins and win it. Because he did not get an automatic ticket into the main tournament, he played through the whole competition alongside all the amateurs, giving each one a start of 21 points a frame, best score of two. These games were played upstairs in the sports complex and in pretty poor conditions.

This in itself was quite a feat and Alex became something of a hero by playing through all the rounds and qualifying. He was now part of the amateur scene. Although of course he was a professional, all the people there took to him because he had taken the effort to come up and qualify. I remember one particular game he played against Bill Kelly, who has now turned professional himself. Bill had a 21 point handicap per frame and after the first was 108 points ahead on aggregate. Amazingly Alex fought back and snatched victory on the final black. There was uproar after the match; it was all about Alex. He then beat Ray Reardon 4–0 in the competition proper and everyone was saying, 'Up Pot Black. Higgins is beating everybody; he should be in Pot Black.'

Alex was now riding high and got through to the final to play me. That morning I had beaten Dennis Taylor in the semi-final. I had just won the last frame to make it 4–1, turned round and who should be facing me there but Alex, who had just won on the other table. I did not know the fellow at all then, not to talk to. He said to me, 'Do you fancy doing something with the prize money?' At that time the winner picked up £1500 and there was £500 for the runner-up.

Naturally I was so chuffed to be in the final I could not care what happened. I said, 'Yes, I don't mind. What do you want to do?' And I remember him saying, 'Do you want to save yourself £250?' I thought for a moment. Altogether there was £2000 in the kitty, so I said, 'No, we'll have £1000 each.' That was it. He agreed. We both wanted to win the tournament, Alex for obvious reasons as much as I did. For me it was the biggest occasion of my life so far.

The match itself was more important to me for that reason than for the actual result, although of course I was trying desperately hard to win – and so was Alex. In fact I won the first two frames and looked as though I might go away from him. But we ended the afternoon at 3–all. In the evening I only won one frame, which gave Alex victory by 7–4. He had played very well against me.

That final was my first experience of a big crowd. There were 2,500 people watching the match and you could not even get away from the table to go to the toilet, the crowds were packed in so deep. It was nothing to do with me, of course, but because Alex was playing. Normally at Pontins everybody wants the amateur to beat the professional. But that day a lot of people were on Alex's side because of what had happened with the Pot Black incident.

I remember coming in for the evening session in a dress suit, looking down and seeing all the people and thinking: God, this is where I want to be. It was the most fabulous experience of my life. All those people and I was going to play a match in front of them. Despite the fact that it was against Alex, I was very confident. I have always been confident in my own ability, although equally I have always had a great deal of respect for my opponents' ability as well. So I have never got to the stage of being over-confident or starting a match thinking: I'm going to beat that fellow. There is a world of difference between that and saying: I'm going to win that match. Against Alex, it was just a great honour to play him.

A lot of my friends told me after the game that I should never have shared the money. I have often thought about that since and would probably now agree with them. But that night I walked off with £1000, which was a bloody fortune. It was my first experience of making big money out of snooker, on the strength of which Annette and I moved to a modern semi-detached house in Swiss Valley in Llanelli. We paid £9,500 for that. And the £1000? Well, when we got back we put it on the mantelpiece for a while and just left it there. And every time I went home I used to see it and think: God, £1000 just for playing snooker. It was unbelievable to me.

Although I would never consider sharing prize money now, I have no regrets about doing it then. I know a lot of people tend to think that if you share prize money then you are not going to try. But that is stupid, because you are there to win the tournament; the money is only an extra. The comment has also been made that I would have put more pressure on Alex by saying no. Had I given it more thought at the time, I may not have agreed to do it. But even the thought of £1000 was too much for me to turn down.

At that time, the professionals came straight from the World Championship, which used to be played in Manchester before it was moved to Sheffield, to compete at Pontins. And I remember looking at Ray Reardon and Graham Miles, two of the top players then, and thinking: They're earning a fortune here – a few thousand pounds for a week's work. My next thought was that I could never imagine myself earning that sort of money. But then it went through my mind that if I played well, I was sure I could give some of the professionals a good run for their money – and I had just proved it – albeit with a 25 point start.

Watching that final was the legendary Joe Davis. It was the only time I ever met the great man and you can imagine the thrill for me just to shake his hand. It is hard to explain really. To most people in snooker Joe at that time was God. I had never seen him play, but I looked at him sitting there watching me – a local amateur from Llanelli and the great Joe Davis watching. It was a wonderful moment. Looking back, I realised then I had the temperament. Some people, with Joe sitting there watching them play, would have gone to pieces. But it gave me an extra incentive to play well.

There again, I think back to the earlier days of competing on the Welsh national scene. I never played in my home town of Llanelli. It was always up in the Valleys against crowds that were very much on the side of the home player. That was a great grounding for me. I was up against that all the time. Every match I had to go and beat better players than me on their own tables, with their own crowd behind them, and I learnt a lot from it. It used to spur me on when I heard them cheering and saying 'good shot' when I missed – and that type of thing. I made me into a hard match player and gave me that extra edge I needed to win the game or play better.

It was the same with Joe Davis and the 2499 other people. I had never experienced such an audience before. I had played in front of hundreds back at home, but nothing like this. And out of the vast crowd there, 1000 of them were the best snooker players – amateur and professional – in the country. And I was actually playing snooker, knowing that all these players were watching me. A lot of people would say: 'God, there are too many good players watching me. Ray Reardon is there watching.' And they could not pot a ball. For me it was quite the opposite. I found it used to give me a real kick.

I shall always remember during that match Joe making a comment to me about Alex's play. Now Alex was all the rage at the time. He was coming to the table and playing extraordinary shots that had never been seen before. Being the perfectionist he was, Joe said to me, 'I don't know what the hell Higgins is trying to do. I don't know how he plays the game.' Alex was so unorthodox, but at the same time so exciting.

That final against Alex was a very hard match. But it was just what was needed. It was Alex when he wanted so desperately to win. There has been the other side, when he would play to the crowd and lose. But to win that Pontins tournament meant so much to him – to give Pot Black a real kick up the backside. Particularly in the second session, he played so hard; there were no breaks for me. He kept me out, which was exactly what a professional should do against an amateur. That was a very good experience for me and one I have learnt a great deal from.

I recall Ted Lowe, the BBC commentator, and Sidney Lee were watching that night. They were both part of the Pot Black set-up and had a very big say in the game at the time. The reason for this was that if you were invited to compete in Pot Black then, you had made it in the professional world. There is no doubt it was the thing. If you got on Pot Black, you got bookings. At that stage there was very little snooker on television. Even when the World Championship was on, only the highlights were ever shown. So really it was all about Pot Black – and that was why the Higgins situation caused so much stir at the time.

My feelings about the Pot Black competition were to crystallise a few years later when I was on the board of the sport's governing body – the WPBSA. But my view of it, I think, stems from this time. It actually dictated what happened to a player's future. I never liked the scene; it was a closed shop, without a shadow of a doubt. You got on Pot Black if the odd place became available. And you got it by favours rather than ability. As an amateur I never liked the gloss of it all, either. What with all the show and the presentation, it was a bit too heavy for me. But I loved to sit and watch the professional players then. I kept meaning to go to the World Championship. But, believe it or not, I never saw a ball struck in that tournament until I played in it myself. I just could not afford it. It was a week before Pontins' and that always took all my money. Annette would come to Prestatyn with me and we would go back home with nothing in our pockets – and the inevitable bills waiting for us. So I never did get to the World Championship as a spectator, although I would have loved to. Mind you, when I did finally make it to The Crucible in Sheffield, what an occasion it turned out to be.

7 Taking the Plunge

WITH THE EXPERIENCE I gained at Pontins and the insight it had briefly given me into top level snooker, I was again considering the implications of turning professional. Having watched and competed against some of the best players in the world, now I started looking at the money side of snooker. Of course they were better than me, but not that much better. Perhaps I could improve my play that bit and begin earning that sort of money. Just think, with the World Championship and the Pontins Open, prize money totalled some £10,000 for two weeks' snooker! Winning that amount, I would have felt a millionaire. But I delayed my decision till the following year.

When it came round, I again found myself in the final of the English Amateur Championship and successfully defended my title against Joe Johnson. But I was given a nasty shock in the very first round by a little-known Devonian called Tony Marsh. He played the game of his life and took me all the way to 4–3. The Southern Area final was an all-Welsh affair. I played Cliff Wilson from Tredegar, who although he was the current Welsh champion never did himself justice in the match. I beat him 8–2.

So it was up to Blackpool to face Joe, who had been in tremendous form and was well fancied for the title. After the 13–6 defeat I inflicted on him, he said to Peter Francis who as usual was up there with me, 'I don't know what I've got to do to beat Terry. I've been playing so well.' But that day I had felt unbeatable.

It was enormously satisfying to have won the English for the second year running. But now came the crunch. The next World Amateur Championship was not until 1980 – two years away. Should I wait another year and hope to qualify by winning the

Welsh again? Or should I now take the plunge and go professional? Annette and I discussed the matter at length.

Of course, the money would be nice, but to earn the right money I would have to be successful. Being successful meant I would be away from home a lot, which really I did not want to happen. I have always been very much a family man and at that time was looking after my two boys alongside the insurance job while Annette was out working. If I was not successful, then there was no point in turning professional. It was a Catch 22 situation.

After much thought and heart-searching, I finally decided in March of that year to apply for professional status. I also made up my mind to give it three years – and even that was going to be hard since there were only a few major tournaments in those days from which you could earn reasonable money. If it did not work out, then I would simply go back to work again. But at least I would have tried. I lost a lot of sleep in the meantime, I can tell you. It was a big decision for me to make because basically I was still the local lad from Llanelli who so far really had not experienced very much of life. Although I had been round the snooker circuit a fair bit by now, I was still very much an amateur player and there is a whole world of difference in the professional game. I spoke to a lot of other players about it, too, and they all said give it a go.

In the end, what really hit home to me and made up my mind was that I was now thirty years old and I did not want to get to forty and be thinking: Would I have done well as a professional? There were a lot of amateur players at that time – very good ones – who had not taken the plunge and who had afterwards said to me, 'When Spencer and Reardon turned professional in the late Sixties, that's when we should have done it, too.'

I looked at them and thought: They're marvellous players; I wonder if they would have made it. I decided I never wanted to get into that position of 'if only . . .' Really, that is what made my mind up – nothing else. It was certainly not just the money. I wanted to pitch my skills against the best players in the world and see if I could beat them.

Having been accepted by the WPBSA in June, I chucked in my job with the Pearl Insurance in August. That in itself caused considerable problems, because we had our house mortgage with them at just four per cent. That immediately shot up to around ten per cent and therefore was costing a lot more money every month. Annette was working at Morris Motors to pay the bills and I was in charge of the kids, getting them to school in the morning and fetching them back in the afternoon. This gave me valuable time for practising, which I had never done as an amateur. I never used to practise that much. So I set myself a goal to play for four hours every day.

The next problem was where to practise and I decided to join the Llanelli Conservative Club. It was the ideal place because it was normally fairly quiet in there during the daytime and I could always get a table without interfering with the other members who wanted to play. Having taken Wayne and Darren to school at nine each morning, I went to the club till lunchtime, when it would fill up with members. I collected the boys from school at about three in the afternoon and waited till Annette came home from work at four, before returning to the club for another couple of hours.

The discipline I set myself was very important. Suddenly my game improved dramatically. But there again, I had never practised that much before and it gave me a lot more confidence. I also realised I had more ability than had previously been apparent.

During this valuable period at the club, I had a lot of support from the members. They knew I had just turned professional and would willingly play against me although they knew they would rarely get a shot and spent most of the time putting the colours back on their spots. I was tremendously grateful for their help at the time, although sadly my relationship with the club was to turn sour after I won the World Championship the following year.

In between practising and looking after the boys, I was fulfilling my remaining amateur commitments up till the first professional tournament, which was in September. But I also had to find other ways of earning my living as a snooker player. Of course, outside Wales nobody had ever heard of me – and not that many in Wales had, either! So again I started circulating clubs with the help of Cyril Richards, although this time I was charging £60 a night and not £15.

All in all, I had a very good response, particularly in Wales. Having written round, I used to spend three hours every Saturday and Sunday lunchtime speaking to the club secretaries, which was not always the easiest of jobs. Most of them had never heard of me anyway. They would either turn me down flat or ask me to phone back in a few weeks' time after they had put it to the committee. I was always very efficient and would make a note of all this and phone them back. I think I got much of my work through that, not because of who I was, although naturally I did have some contacts from my amateur days. Sometimes I was getting two or three bookings in a single week and then nothing for the next three. But overall, it kept me reasonably well in pocket, which was fortunate since I earned virtually nothing from tournaments that season – until the World Championship that is.

I was able to supplement this income by selling cues. Cliff Wilson helped me a lot with this. He used to get these cues from the suppliers; they were actually seconds but good value for money. I sold them off at a reasonable price and still made a profit. It was very good of Cliff to do me this favour, since he had already laid out the money to buy the cues but allowed me to pay him when I had sold them.

In the hope of getting more bookings for exhibition matches and shows, I had joined up with ISA, an agency run by Del Simmons, Ray Reardon and John Spencer. A few years earlier they had decided to form a players' booking agency because at the time there was none. I was very grateful they accepted me, since it was the only agency, although of course they must have realised my potential; also my behaviour and appearance were always good and I would not let them down at venues.

The agreement was that they took ten per cent from all my bookings. Unfortunately Del only got me a few during that period, while I might arrange a couple of evenings a week myself and then have to send him the commission from the £60 I earned each time. To be fair to him, I was then still unheard of and also he had a lot more important players to look after at the time. Reardon, Spencer and Higgins, whom he had also signed up, were the big names in snooker and kept him very busy.

After a while I realised perhaps it was not particularly useful being with the ISA because when you are a nobody, nobody can get you work anyway. And after I won the World Championship, suddenly there was more work coming through than I knew what to do with.

Obviously I wanted to get as much experience as possible of the professional circuit early on and entered a few smaller tournaments.

One I played in was the Lucania Pro-Am. Barry Hearn owned that particular chain of clubs at the time and organised the event. It was being staged in the old Matchroom at Romford, a favourite venue of mine since I had won my first English title there. It was not, however, a happy return since I lost 5–3 to Graham Miles.

But that match did have a positive effect in making me realise what had happened to me as a snooker player. The fact was that as an amateur I never played that much. So when I went into a tournament I used to play a lot better. It may have been because I never practised for any length of time and therefore put all my effort into the game itself. I had gone through the whole of my amateur career like that and had been successful. But now I had turned professional, I was practising four hours a day in the Conservative Club in Llanelli and was playing brilliantly – better than ever in my life.

Unfortunately when I went into a match I could not maintain that standard. I was playing superb snooker in practice, to the extent that I never dreamed I could play so well. But when it came to a competition, I could not handle it. So mentally that match against Graham was a significant stepping-stone in my career. Through it I had come to realise how important it was to carry good form in practice through to a match situation. Until then, I had always been a better match player than practice player. The trouble I was now having was that I had mastered the first and in so doing had temporarily lost the second.

There had not been a lot of money involved in that game. For me, it was pride, because I was playing one of the top people in the game and so desperately wanted to impress. I remember I had to change downstairs; in those days it was not a question of staying in hotels because you simply could not afford them. You just drove to the venue, played your game and drove away again. After the match I went back down to this very small office – and then it all came out. 'What the hell am I doing playing snooker like that?' I was really annoyed with myself. Barry was there and could not believe what he heard. We had only met on a few occasions before and he had thought of me as just a quiet Welsh boy who would not say 'bah' to anybody. Then suddenly there I was exploding in front of him.

'If I am going to play like this, I'm not going to bother being a professional. I'm just wasting my time,' I went on. And all these negative thoughts were coming out. The truth was I was so frustrated that I had not played as well as I had done in practice. Barry did not say anything at the time, but later on he told me how depressed he had felt. He must have thought: What the hell is this idiot talking about? Apparently I really got to him. In fact, Barry actually locked up early that night and went home because he felt so depressed.

But this incident served as a very important lesson to me. It made me realise the difference between practising full-time, which can bring your game on so quickly, and matchplay, which can stop it so quickly.

My next important match was against Rex Williams in the qualifying round of the UK Championship, my very first major professional tournament. And what a nightmare it turned out to be. I was full of confidence because my game was going so well in practice and I expected to win easily. Rex was not playing particularly well at that time and although I did not perform to the standard I was capable of I went into an 8–2 lead. Then everything started to go wrong. Gradually he pulled back – 8–3, 8–4, 8–5 – until incredibly the scores were level.

We were both terribly nervous in the last frame, understandably, and it was no surprise when the match finally rested on the last two balls. After Rex had missed the pink, I leapt from my seat to take the next shot. That was a big mistake. I should have taken my time and settled myself for what should have been the killing blow. Instead I rushed into the shot, potted the pink but went in-off with the cue ball. I was horrified. Rex came back on, did the necessary and that was it.

It was a crushing blow – a terrible experience for me in my first professional tournament. If I had won, I would have played Graham Miles in the competition proper and had been looking forward to gaining my revenge. Added to that, the Guildhall in Preston meant the big time. But it was not to be. That defeat was the worst possible thing that could have happened to me at the time, although it taught me a very sharp and timely lesson. I remember phoning home and telling Annette that I had lost. She burst into tears and that started me off as well. Then the South Wales Echo phoned me up for a story and could not believe what had happened. For that matter, neither could I.

Peter Francis was of course watching throughout and told me afterwards that when I was 8–2 up Barry Hearn came up and gave him a cigar. 'Light this,' he said, 'your boy is through, no problem.' And as Peter's cigar disappeared in smoke, so did my hopes of victory.

After that traumatic experience in Romford, I was due to play three days of exhibitions in Eastbourne for John Hughes. The last thing in the world I felt like was playing those matches. But the crowd in Eastbourne made me very welcome and by the end I had partly got over the disappointment. But it took me several months to forget about it completely. My confidence certainly dropped because of that defeat, although I am sure overall it made me a stronger player. In many ways, Rex did me a big favour and, without knowing it at the time, probably set me up for what was to be my greatest triumph the following spring.

8 That Magic Moment

STRANGELY ENOUGH THERE was no real build-up to my first World Championship in 1979. Apart from a minor tournament I played before the previous Christmas, I did not have a proper match until the preliminary round in March against Bernard Bennett, who curiously had arranged that earlier competition at his Castle Club in Southampton.

In fairness, it did provide me with some useful preparation, if only to help me build up my confidence after that disastrous start to my first professional season. I began by beating Geoff Foulds, then took revenge on Rex Williams – although at 3–3 in a seven-frame match history might well have repeated itself. My next victim was Bill Werbeniuk, but I then lost to his fellow Canadian Cliff Thorburn.

It was obviously very important for me to get through the qualifying rounds of the World Championship and I had already made up my mind that if I did not get through I was going to go back to work and become just a part-time professional.

My match with Bernard was at the Romiley Forum in Stockport. I remember well arriving in the carpark and noticing this man walking in my direction. I recognised him straight away; it was Peter Dyke, who looks after the snooker for Embassy, the tournament sponsors. As he walked past, I said, 'Hello, Peter. You won't remember me. My name's Terry Griffiths. I met you at the first professional players meeting I went to.' Peter looked blankly at me, said, 'Oh yes' and carried on. Of course, we have got to know each other very well since and he always reminds me of that occasion. At the time he was thinking: Who the hell's that guy? A few weeks later he knew. Then I was champion of the world, having just won his tournament.

I got off to a bad start against Bernard, losing the first two frames.

But I went on to beat him quite comfortably, which meant playing Jim Meadowcroft in the qualifying round. Jim has always been a very useful player without making any real impact on the game. But I was confident of winning and so it turned out. The final score was 9–6, although to his credit Jim had come back several times in the match and in fact had levelled the scores at 6–6

Mario Berni, who had played a very important part in my early development as an amateur in Wales, was watching that match and told me later of a conversation he had with someone sitting next to him. The chap had asked him if he knew who I was and where I came from. When Mario told him, he said, 'That man's going to be the next world champion.' I do not know to this day whether that had been an inspired guess or whether he knew something that I did not. But it is certainly nice to know that he, for one, got it right.

Having qualified now for the championship proper, I was happy I had put the Rex Williams nightmare well and truly behind me. There were only two main professional tournaments in those days and I had now got through the qualifiers for the second. This was a great time for me. Not only had I won through to the televised stages at The Crucible, but equally important I had won £1000 for qualifying. And at that time every £1000 was paying something off, not least the Fiat car I was now driving round in. I was so excited and really enjoying my snooker. Everything seemed to be happening for me at last.

I was now eagerly awaiting the draw for the first round, which used to take place live on Saturday Grandstand. In those days only sixteen players got to The Crucible, not like today when it is the last thirty-two. At this stage there were eight seeded players and eight qualifiers and they picked out one of each in turn. Ray Reardon, as defending champion, was the Number One seed and Perrie Mans Number Two as last year's runner-up.

Coincidentally I had arranged for Perrie to play several exhibition matches in Wales just after the New Year and had beaten him on the three nights I played him. When the draw was being made, as you can imagine I was sitting at home glued to my set. There were plenty of players I did not want to draw. I certainly did not want Ray Reardon, for a start. With just four names left, mine still had not come out and nor had Ray's or Perrie's. The next one was mine, followed by the Number Two seed, and I remember jumping up and down, thinking how lucky I had been. I meant no disrespect to Perrie. Of course it was still going to be a hard match for me. But compared to Reardon . . . well, I knew he would just have overwhelmed me. I had got as good a draw as I could have wished for and having recently played and beaten Perrie helped too. My practice was going really well; everything was running smoothly; and when I arrived in Sheffield I was in great spirits.

I shall never forget walking into The Crucible for the very first time. It was like walking on air, just to be there. In many ways my attitude then could best be summed up by a little incident that happened just before the tournament started. I was practising on a table when Bill Werbeniuk came in. He asked how long I was going to be because he wanted to get on himself. I passed a casual remark back, which did not impress him one little bit. In fact Bill told me later what he had been thinking. 'Who's this cheeky thing? He's only just qualified. I wish I had got him in the first round.' He laughed with me about it after I had won.

The BBC had scheduled to film part of the championships over the bank holiday period, which particularly thrilled me because my match against Perrie was due to be covered. That was very important since national television exposure would, among other things, mean lots more bookings. So I was horrified to hear that a strike had been called for that weekend. It suddenly hit me that if I did not beat Perrie, I would not get on television. You can imagine my huge relief when the news came through that the dispute had been settled. I was now in tremendous mood – exactly the right frame of mind for my match with Perrie.

Although the result was never really in doubt after I had taken an 8–2 lead, my inexperience in major tournament snooker and the length of the game did take its toll. I was feeling very tired by the end of the evening session, having played 17 frames – more through the mental effort of having to concentrate for so long. In fact Perrie took the last three frames that night to reduce the deficit to 10–7. Although he pulled another back at the start of the third session, I was by then feeling rested and quite refreshed and settled the match in the next three frames. I was over the moon. Winning through had been a real bonus.

I am not a particularly superstitious person, but I did succumb at Sheffield over a rather bizarre incident the day before. I had left my car parked under some trees alongside the St George Hotel, where I was staying. That morning when I went down to drive to The Crucible, the car was covered in pigeon droppings. Now that Fiat was my pride and joy and I was pretty annoyed. Unfortunately I did not have time to clean the mess off and drove it as it was. After beating Perrie I decided it must have been a lucky omen and so for the rest of the tournament I religiously parked the car under the same trees. As you can imagine, by the end it was literally plastered in droppings.

Now I was due to meet Alex Higgins and what a match it turned out to be. Obviously I am biased, but it has generally been regarded by all who saw it as one of the finest ever in the history of the championship. Even BBC's snooker producer Nick Hunter later agreed that it was one of the greatest games he had televised. Unfortunately that recording has since been mislaid!

The standard of play throughout was tremendous. Alex was playing out of his skin – and so too was I. After the first session he led 6–2 and had made two century breaks. But by the end of the evening I had come back with a strong finish to level the scores at 8–8, winning the last three frames – including a 121 break in the 15th.

The following day in the final session we matched each other frame for frame until I took the advantage at 12–11 and needed just one of the last three frames. By now the tension in The Crucible was unbelievable. Although I did not know it at the time, Annette had come up to see the match and was sitting with my father and Peter Francis in the auditorium. It is just as well I won not only that match but eventually the title, since Annette had chucked in her job because they would not give her time off to come and watch me.

At 12–11, the tension of it all was just too much. She had left her seat and was standing outside in the foyer. Suddenly there was a tremendous roar. Peter appeared through the exit doors and she shouted, 'Has he won, then?' Peter explained that Alex had levelled it again at 12–12 and they both returned to watch the deciding frame. I could not believe my luck when Alex gave me an early chance. I gritted my teeth. This was it. I was not going to let it slip now. John Pullman was commentating at the time and summed up what happened next pretty accurately. 'The boy's really feeling in the pink.' And I was. I played off the pink ball and made a 107 break. That was it, I had won and the whole audience stood up and cheered. What a fantastic moment.

In all the euphoria, however, I did feel sorry for Alex. He had played brilliantly, but equally I had played snooker as well as I think I shall ever play. What made it worse was that prior to the tournament he had stopped drinking alcohol and had gone on to tea. He had put so much effort into packing up the booze and then along comes this new professional, plays the best game of his life and knocks him out. After the match I heard him say, 'F . . . the tea; I'm going back to something stronger now.'

On reflection, there is no doubt in my mind that the victory over Alex mentally won me the championship. I then knew I could go all the way. Beating Perrie had been great, but Alex was top of the tree next to Reardon, really, and I had beaten him on form. Even if I had lost that last frame, I would have been over the moon. I had played under pressure against one of the best in the world. The reason I had turned professional was to see if I could do that. Now I had done it, I felt so good.

Eddie Charlton was now tournament favourite, followed by Dennis Taylor and John Virgo. The other big names had all been knocked out. Significantly it was Eddie who was under the pressure in my next match; certainly it was not me. As you would expect, that semi-final was an epic match that went on until about 1.40 in the morning of the third day! And it was definitely a contrasting game to the previous one against Alex. Eddie's style was methodical, deliberate and calculated. If you are not careful, he can easily mesmerize you – particularly with the preparation he takes for each shot.

I got off to a good start and was 2–0 up with a 101 break in the second frame. By the end of the first evening I held a narrow 4–3 lead. The next day we battled away for five hours on just seven frames in the first session, by when I was 10–4 in front. As the match wore on, I could feel myself losing concentration and my eyes were getting very tired. Eddie took six frames on the trot and I was resigned to losing the last of the evening. But I hung on for an 11–10 lead overnight.

The following day the drawn-out pattern of play continued. By the beginning of the final evening session I had increased my advantage to 15–13, although in taking that last frame Eddie had been given a vital boost, which he capitalised on that night. He won the first three frames to go ahead for the first time in the match at 16–15. He held his lead at 17–16 and now the pressure was well and truly on. If he got the next I would have to win the last three frames. Fortunately I took it, which was a terrible blow for Eddie, and followed this with a 69 break. Now I was one frame off the final. And what a frame it turned out to be. I was trailing 48–0 and had hardly been up to the table. Incredibly, as the excitement around me mounted, I took the last nine reds, seven blacks, two pinks and all the colours – a 97 clearance and a place in the final.

The ovation that followed was out of this world. I was still trying to get to grips with the situation when Peter Francis burst out of the crowd, picked me up and swung me round and round. And when David Vine came over to interview me, I really did not know what to say. After the usual comments about how tough an opponent Eddie was and what a tight struggle it had been, the questions stopped and I stood there exhausted but very happy. 'I'm in the final, now, you know,' I said. Not the most profound words ever spoken, but what can you expect at nearly two in the morning? It had suddenly sunk in what had happened. I could hardly believe it myself.

After the elation of that semi-final, I remember one of the press coming up to me and saying, 'Do you realise you're going to become a star now?' Although I just wanted to laugh in his face, because this had not registered at all with me, I resisted the temptation. I was playing snooker and great . . . I had won. Of course that meant more money. But I had no idea the effect it would have with the people watching at home. Now they had someone they could relate to. I had just recently come out of a job and was playing the best in the world and it seemed the nation as a whole was coming over to my side, as they tend to do in such situations.

And because I gave straightforward, honest answers at the many interviews, I think this helped my image with the people a lot. It overrode the fact that I was playing very slowly at the time. Nobody seemed to care, really, as long as I was winning. I was not conscious of it until I watched the tapes afterwards. My play really was painfully slow at times – worse than ever before or after. And people tend to forget that. I have been criticised at lot in recent years for the time I take over my shots, but I have never been as slow as I was in that championship. Because I was the new boy, the crowd's hero, somehow it was all right.

Without meaning any disrespect to Dennis Taylor whom I have become very friendly with since, the final that meant more to me at that time than anything in the world was somewhat of an anti-climax from a snooker point of view. I had had two fabulous matches – first against Alex and then against Eddie – so in a way it was almost inevitable that my final game with Dennis was going to fall short of both.

By current day standards the final was a potential marathon, the best of 47 frames over three days, which to me seemed and was an enormous battle. I had never been involved in anything as long as that before and prior to the match I would have been quite happy to settle for level scores going into the final day, when I could concentrate on my game for the last, deciding frames. And so it turned out to be.

On the first day I had taken a 5–2 advantage but again fell victim to growing tiredness by the end of the evening, when I led 8–7. Strangely enough, the second day was probably the worst of the whole championship for me. I was none too pleased with my play and twice Dennis took the advantage – at 11–9 and again at 14–12. But he seemed to go off the boil at that stage and at the end of the scores were level at 15–15.

We had reached the point of no return. It was the last day of the championship, by the end of which the world title would be decided. Very often the opening frame of a session can set the tone for the rest of that period and so it was for me. Having won that vital frame to put myself 16–15 ahead, I never looked back. When we went into the final session I was 22–16 ahead and needed just two more frames for glory. I took them both, the last with a final break of 56.

I vaguely remember Dennis coming straight over and shaking my hand. That was a fine gesture. At that moment there were more emotions in the audience than down by the table. Annette and my father were both in tears. Peter offered my wife a handkerchief and said, 'Cry your eyes out, Annette. You're a rich woman now.' Two weeks earlier I had been a nobody. Now I was champion of the world, as David Vine announced to millions of viewers. I hardly heard him saying it, because by this stage I had gone completely. The snooker was over. There was nothing more to do – or say.

Back in the dressing room, I could hardly believe what had happened. I just sat there and cried with joy. I could not stop it.

Traditionally after the end of the championship the finalists and their wives were invited to a special dinner with the sponsors. I had left my car at the hotel, so Dennis offered to drive us all there. As I walked out to his car, holding the trophy, I said, 'Do you mind putting the cup in the boot?' I did not think anything of it. But poor Dennis did not like it at all. Talk about rubbing salt in the wounds – I had just beaten him in the final and now I was asking him to carry the trophy!

After dinner we were all taken off to a local nightclub, which was the first time Annette and I had been in such a place. That is the other side of the professional's life that I do not particularly enjoy. It was all so strange to me, although I was to realise very much part of the price you had to pay for being a world champion.

When we finally got back to our hotel, there was a bottle of champagne sitting on the table for us – from Del Simmons. And even when we woke up later that morning there was no peace. The press wanted to take a picture of Annette and me in bed. Suddenly it hit home to me what my victory really meant. I had become a star overnight, not just because I had won the World Championship but the circumstances in which I had done it.

We had been up in Sheffield now for two weeks and all Annette and I wanted to do was to go home to see the boys and the rest of the family. But before that I had the annual meeting of the WPBSA to sit through. This is traditionally held the morning after the World Championship final. Poor Annette had to hang around all day while the meeting went on – and by the time it finished, after ten hours, it was too late to get back to Llanelli. So we had to wait till the following morning.

It is very strange, as they say, what a difference a day makes. Before, I used to sit in a corner with the rest of the players and what views I might have held meant little at all. Then I won a tournament and suddenly everyone was taking notice. For some reason my views had now become important. It only goes to show how false the world can be sometimes. I did stick with the WPBSA as a committee member for more than three years and must admit enjoyed getting involved in the organisation of the game and trying to improve it. But on that particular occasion there was really only one thought in my mind. I wanted to be back home – in Llanelli.

9 A Different World

ANNETTE AND I finally arrived home from Sheffield with a great sense of relief – and bewilderment. I suppose I had not really thought about the fact that there would be those in Llanelli who wanted to add their congratulations and organise a typically Welsh reception. When we got there a tremendous crowd had gathered to greet us, particularly around the house. Rows of flags stretched from the rooftops and I can still see the huge banner with 'Welcome home champ' in large red letters. That scene really brought it home to me how much support I had got from my own town. They had been following the events of the last two weeks so closely that when there had not been any television coverage, they had been jamming The Crucible's switchboard to find out the latest score.

It was a marvellous but very strange experience. I had had all the bright lights in Sheffield and could handle that. But now I was back in Llanelli, outside my own house, where it is normally quiet and peaceful. Suddenly there were all these people everywhere – aunts, uncles, neighbours, friends . . . And there, in among the crowd, was Steve Davis.

I had previously booked Steve to come down and play a couple of shows before the end of the championship, not realising or believing I would last that long. Because I was still in Sheffield, Steve had stayed with our next-door friends Susan and Jeff. And there he was – unrecognised – just another face in the crowd. We have had a few laughs about that since.

When we finally got indoors, there was a constant stream of well-wishers coming in and out. It was an amazing feeling, although without meaning to sound ungrateful I just wanted to sit down and have a cup of tea. I had not seen the kids for a few weeks, either, and wanted to spend some time with them. Because I had spent the best part of the last year looking after them, we had grown very close and I did not want them to feel left out of all that had happened. Obviously they were caught up in the general excitement without really knowing why and were necessarily involved in the aftermath, such as when the BBC came down and filmed the family. But I suspect it took some time for them to feel the full effect of having a celebrity as a father.

After all the excitement had died down, it was back to work. My first engagement was at the Kilgetty Club in Pembroke, a booking I had made some months previously. Although I was now world champion and could of course command a much greater fee, there was no way I would not fulfil my earlier commitments – even at £60 a night! I doubt there was anywhere in Wales that had followed my progress in Sheffield more closely. Every time I won a match at The Crucible, the club rang up to check that I was still coming to play. That in itself was very flattering for me, as was the staggering amount of mail I received during that fortnight. There were telegrams, cards and letters by the box-full. The public's reaction was overwhelming.

I drove to Kilgetty with David Hopkin, who worked for Billiards & Snooker Wales and had been a great help in organising bookings for me over this period. With all the excitement after The Crucible, I had not touched my cue and from a playing point of view was slightly concerned that I might let them down on the night. We turned off the main road into the street leading to the club and, well . . . it was just fabulous. We felt like royalty driving through the crowd with everyone waving and cheering.

That night, everyone wanted to be in the club and the reception they gave me was quite incredible. The fact that I was so overcome and could not play to save my life did not seem to matter. They were so pleased to have me there – and equally I was proud to be there.

What came home to me more than anything else was that I had never thought or expected something like this to happen. Suddenly I realised what the events of those two weeks in Sheffield had meant not just to me but from a Welsh point of view as well. It was a wonderful feeling.

That evening in Kilgetty provided me with an early taste of the good things that were to come from my success. Unfortunately there was another, less happy side which I should have anticipated but, as is only natural, was slightly shaken by when it came.

Shortly after I got back home, I decided to call in at the Llanelli Conservative Club to say thank you to everybody for helping me prepare for my eventual world title triumph. I walked in as usual through the large lounge on my way to the snooker-room. It took me nearly two hours to get through, since everyone wanted to talk to me. It was a marvellous gesture and I happily stopped to chat. Finally I got through to the snooker-room to see all the people I had been practising with over the previous months.

Everyone was clapping and suddenly I got a big lump in my throat. It was all getting a bit heavy for me. Instinctively I went and put my name up on the board, as I had done so many times before. I thought that having a game with the lads would divert attention off me for a bit. Unfortunately that proved to be a fatal mistake. One of the boys playing saw me doing it, turned to everyone there and said, 'Oh look, it's the world champion putting his name up on the board. Well, I'm not coming off the table for him.' There was a deathly hush. Well, that just did my head in. He obviously did not realise the harm he had done. All I wanted was to have a game with the lads. But he had mistakenly interpreted it as me throwing my weight around. There was no point in trying to explain. The damage had been done. I turned round and walked out. And I have never been in the club since.

That served as a perfect example of how attitudes had changed among people whom I used to meet and mix with on a regular totally informal basis. Now I was starting to hate the whole situation. There were people talking to me now who had never spoken before and equally those who used to talk who did not anymore. I remember afterwards Peter Francis told me that people in the Conservative Club were saying that I was too big for the place now. I just could not believe or understand this. And it hurt.

People were thrilled I had won, but equally there was a lot of jealousy of my success and a lot of rumours, which I suppose you can understand in a small community like Llanelli. People were saying that I had changed now that I had got money and fame. Of course I freely admit that my lifestyle was changing because I had been thrown into a completely different world. But there was no way I – Terry Griffiths – had changed as a person. But things like that were to change me quickly and make me much harder towards other people.

In the weeks and months that followed, Annette and I were to become even more aware of how our life was being changed by circumstance without us being able to do anything about it. We would ring old friends we had not seen since Sheffield and they would say, 'Well, people would think we were hanging on if we came down to the house.' I thought: Christ, you're old friends. But even they were looking at us differently. On one occasion Annette and I went out with two of our best friends. After the meal I went to pay, which was a mistake. I wanted to pay – and a few weeks earlier would have offered just the same without any problem. But they turned round and said, 'Why should you pay for our meal?' Now they were looking at us differently. I just did not know what to do. If I did not pay I would have been accused of being tight. If I did pay they would say I was a flash bastard.

The nett result of all this was that sadly but inevitably I began to break away from my roots in the town. I found I could no longer go into Llanelli. When I did, particularly with the family, people would stop me for a chat, because they were thrilled to see me. While it was very flattering, it was not fair on Annette and the boys who would just have to walk on and leave me there. This really started to hurt since it was driving a wedge between us, so I stopped going into Llanelli for a while. Suddenly we were having to put ourselves into a shell, in a place that I loved, a place that had always been my home.

On top of all this, I was faced with the depressing thought of having to go away to fulfil my commitments. All this was building up inside me at a time when I should have been enjoying my success and achievements. I felt I had been pushed into a corner with no way out.

The truth of our new situation really came home to me a while afterwards when I was driving to town with Wayne, my eldest boy, in the Mercedes. Some kids noticed me and all started waving. I said to Wayne, 'I just can't get used to being recognised like this.' 'Well, if I saw a big sports car I'd be waving like that too,' he replied. That put it all in context for me. Wayne could not see me any differently because he was my son. But everyone else did. It took a kid to say that to me before I recognised it.

I then realised that I would have to change my life to get used to this and so I became more of a recluse. It did not affect me professionally, which was quite surprising. Once I packed up the car and went out of the drive, I was in another world. I was a different person – from husband and father into a sports personality. Of course, this was bound to be the biggest year of my life – and Annette's as well. The change in such a short space of time was dramatic. And it was not a question of saying I handled it all right. I did not handle it at all. It just happened.

As far as snooker was concerned, the effect of being world champion was naturally quite dramatic. All of a sudden my diary was full up. My original intention had been to keep so many days free to spend at home and with the family, but that of course proved impossible. And because of my heavy commitments at this time, I very nearly fell foul of the Llanelli and District Snooker League.

What happened was that some of the League officials had suggested that they should fix a night at which they collected entrance money and use it to buy me a present for winning the world title. It was a very warm and generous thought. Apparently they collected over £300 and when they went to Harry Cass, a local jeweller, to buy the gift, he said he would double the amount. They bought a set of cufflinks with gold sovereigns with the money – a truly fine present.

I was involved in a match at the Fishers Cub one night, when the Secretary of the League, Len Jones, came up to me and told me that they had arranged a presentation evening at the Trostre Club. I explained to him that I would of course be delighted to come, but I could not guarantee the date, since I had so much on. Not one to mince his words, Len replied, 'Well, it's all fixed so you bloody better be there.' As it turned out, I was able to go, although the feeling at the club was that I was trying to snub the members. That simply was not true. I was pleased to be there and very touched by their generosity and kindness.

For that summer of 1979, I had already negotiated a contract with Butlins to appear at the Clacton and Skegness holiday camps. The original five days' work, which was worth £170, was a great thing for me to get. It meant money in the summer, which before now I had needed desperately. But because I had won the world champion-ship, Butlins now wanted to change the arrangements and, I hasten to add, pay me more money. It was agreed that I would appear at all eight of the camps over a two-week period for £355 a week. Since I would otherwise have had to stick to the original contract, I was quite happy with the change.

The trouble was that I had not taken into consideration how much work I was now going to get. What with the Butlins job and the other appearances I had to fit in, each time I left the house I was up to my eyes in complicated itineraries. These could involve me in a seven-hour drive to one venue, an overnight stop then off again to another venue, in between fitting in a company promotion . . . and so it went on. If I was lucky I might over a fortnight get a day at home – and even then I would have to spend most of that sorting out paperwork, seeing my accountant or looking after more personal matters such as visits to the dentist.

The response I got from playing Butlins was tremendous. I remember going to Skegness, where the snooker-room was a 100 metre square greenhouse, with about forty tables. I was pushing the door to get in but could not open it for all the people that had packed in to see me. It was such a thrill, such an experience. And they were all cheering and clapping. It was quite overwhelming and words cannot describe how I felt. That kind of experience really made all those long journeys worthwhile. Even Butlins admitted it had never experienced anything like it before and had to rope off the match table to keep the crowds back. Previously with players like myself appearing you would have had to have dragged a camper out to have a game.

Anyway, when I finally got inside, it was like entering a sauna – all these people and no air-conditioning and I had to play on a table that was literally wet with the heat. I finished playing – about four games – and then we had the autographs. I came out after two hours gasping and sweating, changed and then rushed off to another venue and played that show in the evening before collapsing into another strange bed. Then it was up again bright and early the next day to drive off elsewhere.

Of course, with all this rushing around, there were compensations. Every time I came home, which was not often enough, I would have all this money. It was so strange to me. All of a sudden I felt rich. Because we had started off with virtually nothing when I turned professional, however, it did take quite a time for the money to build. To begin with, everything I got was spent on things we needed. I remember one week coming home with £1000 in my pocket and thinking: This is really worthwhile, you know.

With the thrill of winning the world championship, getting lots of summer work and coming home with the money, everything was going very well – certainly as well as I could have dreamed. But I was missing the children terribly. It was awful. Annette could come with me because she had packed in her job. But the kids were still too small to take round with us. One of the beauties of becoming world champion was that Annette did not have to work anymore, which had always been one of her lifetime ambitions. Now she could look after the boys which she had always wanted to do but had had to leave it to me since we needed her to be out earning as well.

For several years now, Peter Francis had been travelling around with me and sharing the driving. With all the extra work I now had, his help and companionship were even more appreciated. We have had plenty of laughs together during the many thousands of miles we have travelled and one particular incident at this time always sticks out in my mind. It was my first trip to Filey to play at Butlins. Peter was driving at the time while I slept on the back seat. On the way, he woke me up. 'Heh Terry, the police have stopped me. Can you have a word with them?' He thought the police would recognise me and therefore let him off, since he had been caught speeding. All this happened, strangely enough, on the M62 just a few miles from where I had a nasty crash a few months later.

When the policeman came up to the car, Peter said, 'We're from Wales, you know. I'm driving Terry Griffiths up to Butlins at Filey.' The chap smiled, 'That's the trouble with you Welshmen. You're just not used to long straight roads.' I rolled up. What a bloody marvellous thing for the policeman to say at the time. We had a chat, I signed an autograph for his son and Peter was booked. I paid his fine, of course, but he was really annoyed that I had not helped to get him off.

The accident I referred to happened as I was driving from Llanelli to play Jimmy White, then still an amateur, in Scarborough. For events that involve a lot of travel, now I would drive up the day before and stay overnight. But in those days to save on hotel bills I drove up very early straight to the match. This particular morning I was up at some ridiculous hour and had left the house by five.

Annette was in a huff because we had had a big argument the night before. She said afterwards she regretted it and felt very guilty. But I would never blame her for what happened. It was just one of those things. Seeing so little of each other, it must have been very difficult for her at the time.

I drove up through mid-Wales with mist all the way since it was winter time – and my eyes were really tired and aching. I stopped near Chester and had a short rest, then continued the seven-hour journey. I had got near Leeds on the M62 and pulled into a small service area to have another break and a cup of tea. As I drove in, I noticed the lorry park was full and, because I was then very nervous of going into crowds of people by myself, I thought: I haven't got long to go now. I'll carry on. So off I went, opening the window to get some fresh air, and had been driving about ten miles when just outside Leeds I fell asleep. The car hit the side barrier, spun across the road and hit the central barrier – and this bounced it back and forth along the motorway like a tennis ball. Finally the car stopped. I was terribly shaken up and all my clothes, which had come out of the boot, were strewn all down the carriageway. Fortunately, being a Sunday morning, the road was quite quiet. If it had been busy, like on a weekday, there would probably have been the most awful pile-up.

A guy pulled up behind me and said, 'What the hell are you doing?' As if he could not see what had happened! He obviously was pretty shaken up as well. I went to pick up my clothes and thought, 'Let's get off the motorway, quickly.' Luckily I was close to the Junction 31 slip road; so, having put all my stuff back in the car and prised the body off the wheels, I just managed to drive it off the motorway. I phoned to get the car towed away and then rang Annette. She was really upset and burst into tears because she thought it had been her fault. I explained that it was just me trying to do too much, which was right. It was a sharp and timely lesson about driving when you are over-tired.

I think that day must have been destined for disaster from the start. I rang the venue, the Stephen Joseph Theatre, and the promoter Alan Armstrong said he would pick me up. On the way his car broke down and he had to hitch a lift to get to me. We then got a lift to the Crest Hotel in Leeds. If it had not been for the kindness of a chap who had approached me for my autograph, we would have been in real trouble. He packed his family off in a taxi and took us the rest of the way to Scarborough. As it was, I arrived just under an hour late for the afternoon session. You can imagine what I thought when I heard Jimmy had not yet arrived. Apparently he believed it was just an evening session!

The people at the club were extremely sympathetic and understanding. We arranged that I played eight members and somehow I got through that, although with the shock of it all I was hardly in a fit state to play anybody. When Jimmy finally turned up I found out that he had bet his fee with the promoter that he would beat me. I was absolutely mad and that inspired me to play really well that evening and beat him.

Later that year I played Jimmy again in an exhibition tournament at the Louth Town and Country Club. Tony Meo was also there and I had agreed to give them both a lift after the event. I remember it was snowing and I was anxious to get away, but could not find them. Eventually Peter Francis and I found them by the fruit machines and literally had to drag them out to the car.

Towards the end of 1979 I decided to finish with ISA. I was not very happy with the way things were working out and Del Simmons was at the time very heavily involved with the idea of forming a rival players body to the WPBSA – the PSA – although this never got off the ground. He was also booking agent for a dozen or so of the top players now and was not getting me any endorsements or bookings that I could not get myself. So I was looking for another agent and had arranged to see Barrie Gill, who runs CSS, at the London office. The day before I was playing in Clacton, then had a show that evening in Billericay. So Peter and I travelled back into London the same night to stay at the Westbury Hotel, where CSS had booked us in.

Now Peter in some respects is typical of us Welsh in that we tend to have a reputation for being very suspicious of anyone from the outside world – especially London. As we were driving into town, he kept saying to me, 'I don't know why you want to meet these people from London. They're all bloody crooks, too posh and too smart by half for my liking.' I smiled. It was a typical Welshman's reaction to my efforts to get on in the world.

When we pulled into the hotel forecourt at about two in the morning, the commissionaire came to greet us. 'Good evening, Mr

Griffiths. If you'd like to leave me the keys and book in, I'll park the car for you.' So Peter and I walked in to this huge reception area, all done up in marble, where there were still a few people having coffee. I went up to reception thinking: This is the business. And while I was checking in, the chap at the desk was saying, 'Hello, Mr Griffiths. Well done on your win.' So, of course, I was feeling on top of the world.

All of a sudden from behind me I could hear the inimitable Welsh tones of Peter and shall never forget those immortal words . . . 'F . . . . .' hell, Terry, have you seen the price of this place?' I just wanted the floor to open up and swallow me, because everyone there had heard what he said. I slinked quietly up to my room with another timely reminder – don't get carried away!

The next morning I was due to meet Barrie Gill at 8.30 to discuss joining up and getting out of my contract with ISA. In the meantime, because the hotel was so expensive, Peter insisted on staying in his room right up till midday to get full value for money. And he took everything he was allowed to out of the room – soap, shampoo, stationery and so on. We had been sleeping in this vast, luxurious suite, which had provided an intriguing contrast to the Butlins chalets we have been staying in the previous three nights. Sooner or later Peter just had to say something about this. And I was not proved wrong. 'I don't know. From Butlins' chalets to the Westbury Hotel! You're getting carried away with all this success, Griffiths.'

As a result of my meeting with CSS, I joined up with Barrie Gill mainly to try and get some commercial endorsements, which had not really been done before by a snooker player. And in fairness to CSS, I did get a few good contracts, despite the fact that at the time snooker players were not the 'in' thing. The market was very limited, even when Barry Hearn started with Steve Davis.

One of the best contracts was with UDT, the finance company, which Mark Wildman was heavily involved with. That meant playing 40 shows around the country in car showrooms, which proved a very successful venture all round. It also meant a tremendous fee – £1000 a night – whereas my normal fee now was £200. For this I had to meet the clients during the day and play at the garage that evening.

The contract ran for a year and was certainly the most enjoyable work I had with CSS. Turning a car showroom into a snooker theatre for the night was quite an achievement in itself and I found myself in some strange situations. I remember one venue in Ipswich where the roof was leaking. Another time I played in a garage workshop, with all these big heaters blowing away. The garages themselves were delighted because they were giving their customers a different night's entertainment. And we had plenty of fun as well, particularly with the lads who travelled round with us putting up the table each time.

Reflecting back on ISA, I did look upon Del as a friend, but equally I needed a change of management. He had been more of a booking agent and I did not think he was quite the right man for what I was looking for out of my snooker success.

However, not a lot happened with CSS, either. There were a few things I got through it, apart from the UDT contract, but its main interest was in getting to take people like myself around and show us off, which personally I did not think was the right approach to take since I was so busy anyway.

One event I have to blame CSS for was my appearance on This Is Your Life, which took place shortly after Christmas. I remember we had just bought our new house in Pembrey and were staying with the in-laws while we waited to move in. The previous day I had been playing in the Wilson's Classic in Manchester, where I was knocked out by Alex Higgins. Then I travelled back down to London because CSS had apparently arranged for me to see some potential sponsors.

It was now about 6pm and I was absolutely shattered, having spent all day with Barrie Gill talking to sponsors. We were driving along a street, allegedly en route to a Ford dealer's showroom to talk about an exhibition, when this bus pulled out in front of us. I noticed this crowd of people on the bus and thought: I know that face. But I could not work out what was happening. Suddenly all these lights came on and I recognised some of the lads from Llanelli. What's going on here? There must be a match or something. Then Eamon Andrews stepped off the bus with the famous 'Red Book' and uttered 'the words'. As they took me back to the television theatre, I was in a total daze. I wanted to see the kids before the show started, but they would not let me.

That night, in the theatre, for the first time in my life I was lost for words. Emotionally it was too much for me. The next thing I knew the show was over . . . and that was it. It all went past me like a dream. Obviously it had taken months to prepare, with Annette, family and friends talking about all the things that had happened. She had had to take valium because she could not stand the thought of being on television. Of course, it was a great honour to be chosen for the programme, but at the time I really could not take it all in. People had said to me before that I would someday get on the show, but I had just laughed at them. I never thought it would happen.

In fact, it very nearly didn't. They almost got caught out because on the morning of the show I rang the in-laws to see how the kids were. Mrs Edwards, the next-door neighbour, answered the phone and I asked if Wayne or Darren were there? No. Tom or Audrey? No, they were all up in London. Now Annette was lying next to me in bed at the time and was having a heart attack all through the conversation. I said to her, 'Mrs Edwards says everyone's in London.' 'No, of course not. She doesn't know what she's talking about. Come on, they're waiting for you downstairs.' And so I was rushed off into a very busy day and thought no more about it. It was a desperately close thing that, because if you find out beforehand, they cancel the programme. I did not realise till afterwards how near I got to blowing it completely.

As well as setting up events like This Is Your Life, CSS was trying to get me to major charity functions in London, tennis matches and other similar occasions to put my name in front of as many people as possible, I suppose. During one visit to London, Barrie Gill had got tickets to the Long Room at Lord's for the Test Match against Australia, in which incidentally Graham Gooch scored a century. Peter Francis was with me and, much to his annoyance, I decided to give it a miss because I wanted to get home. I enjoyed cricket but was not fussed about getting into the 'Holy of Holies'. Peter never forgave me for that.

I felt I should have been doing more things on television, but it was difficult because in those days snooker players were just not heard of. While I was prepared to let CSS carry on trying, I was still doing my own bookings. And even handling just that side kept me extremely busy. Whenever I got home I would have a bundle of mail to sort through and reply to, but fortunately friends locally helped me out with typing letters and so on.

I think the basic problem with my tie-up with CSS was that the agency had many more important clients on its books – much bigger names than I was. For example, there were the Liverpool football team, the English cricket team and stars like Stirling Moss and Daley Thompson and quite frankly I felt lost among that line-up of talent. But I let things run until the beginning of 1982 before I decided to look around again for a change of management.

Looking back on my first year in the top flight as a player, things ended on a very high note in December when I was invited on to BBC's Sports Review of the Year programme. This was a very important show for me because it attracted millions of viewers and all the top sporting personalities were there – including that magnificent Grand National hero, Red Rum. But what an act to follow! I had to come on afterwards and play some trick shots. I was as nervous as anything.

Now the secret of trick shots is, of course, to set the balls up properly. I had decided to do the 'Snake Shot' first, because it was relatively easy. To save time, I had set the balls up on the table next door so I would be ready when they wheeled it in to the main auditorium. The BBC had had this marvellous idea of putting the table on an air cushion about four inches high so it could be moved in without disturbing the levels or anything on it.

After Red Rum had finished, the table was brought in and I was introduced by Frank Bough. When I got to the table, to my horror the balls were all over the place. Now I was panicking. So Frank said, 'What's the first shot, Terry?' I was still busy setting up the snake shot again. I knew I had not got it set up quite as I wanted, but I thought it would be all right. So I played it and the yellow at the end of the snake wobbled in the jaws of the pocket. That was one down and I had three to go. While I set up the next – known as the Grand National which I chose as something very topical – I was relying entirely on my ability to chat to get over the first disaster. Fortunately that one worked. What a relief!

The third trick shot involved jumping the cue ball over the 15 reds, through the triangle and into the far pocket. This was a relatively easy one, as well, but the secret is to hit down on the cue ball. So I tried to get up for the shot, only to realise that the table was now about five inches too high. Apart from the nerves I was experiencing, I could not get the height I wanted. I'm never going to do this, I thought. In the meantime Frank was trying to chat me along.'What's the next shot going to be?' He was, of course, only trying to help, but a lot of viewers thought he was just harrassing me and apparently he got a lot of bad mail about it afterwards. I have done that trick thousands of times at exhibitions, but never was I so pleased to see that ball go in the pocket. I never thought I would get it with the extra inches on the table. I went on and finished my show and it was a tremendous success.

Afterwards I had a few laughs with Frank about what had happened, but at the time I was in a terrible state because I felt it was not me that was on show, but snooker itself. And I did not want to let the rest of the players down. It had, however, given me a taste of the big time in sport in front of so many people and I had eventually performed successfully, which helped me a lot. I often wonder, looking back, what I would have done if I had missed those shots . . . just collapsed, I think.

10 The Year of The Champ

ALTHOUGH MY REIGN as world champion on the professional circuit began and ended in defeat, it did prove very successful financially. Certainly it got underway on a highly enjoyable note, when I went to Canada to play in the Open at Toronto in August. In fact I made the most of the trip, taking Annette and the boys so we could use it as a holiday as well.

The tournament was part of the annual Canadian National Exhibition and took very much a back seat in the priority of events there, which included a funfair, sports, pop concerts, cattle shows, trade exhibits – you name it, they had it. Considering the conditions we had to play under, I feel I did pretty well to get to the final, where I had a tremendous battle with Cliff Thorburn, losing by the odd frame in 33. Obviously it would have been nice to have consolidated my Sheffield victory of four months earlier, but I was not too disappointed in the result.

The arena we played in had no air-conditioning and was as a result roasting hot. Access to it was via an elevator and children used to wander up to look carrying balloons and other souvenirs from the fair downstairs. As you can imagine, the atmosphere in there was quite unbelievable. The tournament was being televised for the first time and there were four spotlights round the table, which not only added to the heat but also meant you could not see a thing because of the glare. They tried to reduce the heat by placing fans near the table. All these seemed to do was blow your hair all over the place when you went to take a shot.

Before that, they used to play the snooker in a huge tent in the centre and Dennis Taylor told me the story of the MC coming on and asking the crowd for peace and quiet to give the players the best possible atmosphere. Then the band struck up in the next-door tent!

After the final, we flew back to Heathrow at breakfast time and I drove the family home. I was due in Leeds that night to play in a small tournament at the Queens Hotel, so I then rushed off to catch an air taxi from Swansea. I had not been to bed for forty-eight hours!

The snooker season really got underway with the first-ever State Express World Cup, which was staged at the Haden Hill Leisure Centre near Birmingham. The Welsh team comprised Ray Reardon, Doug Mountjoy and myself and we had been made favourites for the title. You would not have thought so, however, when in our first match we went 4–0 down to Canada. We eventually won through 8–6 and beat Australia by a similar margin in the next qualifying match after a surprisingly tough struggle.

Interestingly Gary Owen had come into the Australian side as a late replacement for Eddie Charlton. Gary was from a little village called Tumble just outside my home town of Llanelli and had twice won the World Amateur title and had also been runner-up to John Spencer in the 1969 World Professional Championship. Since then he had emigrated and drifted from the scene a bit. But he gave me quite a scare after taking the first frame of our match.

We went on to beat England very easily in the final. The score was 14–3 and neither Fred Davis, John Spencer or Graham Miles played anywhere near the sort of snooker they were capable of. I have to say it was quite an anti-climax, although it did help establish the event, which has over the years become very popular. It was certainly nice to be back on television again and I was pleased about the way I played. I have always felt a lot of pride playing for my country – and that goes back to my earlier amateur days as well. It was therefore a tremendous honour for me to win the BBC Wales Sports Personality of the Year award, which I was presented with in Cardiff the following January during the Benson and Hedges Masters in London. I took the train down to collect my trophy. That provided me with a unique 'double' since I had a month or so back been voted Newcomer of the Year by the Sports Writers Association – the first time it has ever been given to a snooker player.

The next major tournament, in November, was the Coral UK Championship at the Guildhall in Preston. Despite our success in the World Cup. I was still out to prove that my triumph at The Crucible had not been a flash in the pan. There were those who said it had been a one-off and I would not do anything else and I must admit that thought had gone through my mind as well.

My third round victory against Cliff Wilson meant another match with Alex Higgins in the quarter-final. I was quite relieved to have got through, since I was having trouble with my cue tip at the time and kept swapping over and trying to play in different ones. Now I was really keyed up for this match, since Alex had thrashed me 8–1 at an exhibition a few weeks earlier in Tenby and then really annoyed me during a game at the Deeside Leisure Centre in Queensferry, where he won 4–2.

The problem came not with the result but during the period after when I was trying to play some trick shots for the 1000-odd crowd that had come to watch. To appreciate fully the situation, let me put you in the picture. We were in Wales, I as a Welshman was the reigning world champion and everybody wanted me to win. Alex had played exceptionally well that night and beaten me easily. So at least I could give people something to enjoy with my trick shots. But they were not working well – particularly the basket shot at the end, which I just could not do. So Alex jumped up from his chair, came over to the table and said, 'Let me do it.'

Knowing Alex as I do now, I can appreciate that he did it to try and help me out. But everyone was booing him. He had taken the night, done his stuff and beaten me easily. Now people thought he had come out to take over the trick shots as well. I had a few words with him and told him what I thought about it. That night I decided not to play him any more in exhibitions. And I never have since then.

Alex of course told a different story. He claimed I was frightened of playing him. But he never actually came and asked me why I would not play him anymore. So now the rift was formed between us and there was necessarily quite an atmosphere for the match in Preston. There is always atmosphere when Higgins plays, but this was different.

I went 5–2 in front, having played brilliantly. Alex won the next five frames to make it 7–5, but I hit back to take the last four frames and go through to the semi-final. It had been anyone's match, played in very contrasting styles, and without doubt a great match for the spectators. I went backstage afterwards and I knew there was going to be trouble. I locked my dressing room door and could hear Alex through the wall in the adjoining room. I thought I would give him 10 minutes to get out of the way, because I wanted to avoid a confrontation. I have always respected him as a player – the way he fights for everything – but I did not want a fight off the table as well.

Dennis Taylor went into his dressing room and I could hear Alex having a go at him about some cues he owed him from Ireland. He was swearing away. Finally it cooled down. Alex went and I decided to go as well. So I put my head round the door and who was standing there at the end of the corridor but Alex and Henry West, whom I have known for years. Henry, a big fellow and an ex-boxer, used to manage Jimmy White and Tony Meo. Of course, I was stuck now. I could not go back. So I walked down towards Alex, knowing I would have to say something to him. I shook his hand and said, 'That was a great match, Alex. Anyone could have won it.' Back came the reply, 'Why do you always have all the F . . . . .' luck when you're playing against me?' I wanted to tell him to piss off, but restrained myself and said quietly, 'Look Alex, if I had your talent, I'd never lose any matches.'

There was silence. I could see it had floored him and he did not know what to say. I am afraid Alex needs people to tell him these things. I said it then because that was how I felt. Henry West came after me and said, 'How the hell you didn't hit the fellow, I shall never know. It was marvellous.'

Of course Alex and I still talk to each other, but we have never really got on because we are totally different people. I have had so many good games with him, victories and defeats. There have been very few one-sided matches. But win or lose, I have always enjoyed them. And I think he has always respected me as a player, although hated it because I always slow him down.

When I was on the WPBSA committee, I did my best to try to help straighten him out. And at the time I felt you had to be tough with him – whether that involved a fine or a ban. But it never happened properly. There was one meeting in Sheffield – the AGM in 1982, after Alex had won the championship against Ray Reardon. He was up again over a disciplinary matter and someone said, 'You can't ban the world champion. He wouldn't be in the tournaments. What are the sponsors going to say?' So he was let off. The board was too weak. They should stamp their authority – not just on Alex, but anybody. They failed to do it. And the problems continued.

Mum and Dad's wedding day. The family line-up (from the left) is: Grandfather Freddie, Auntie Edie, Dad, Aunt Jenny, Mum, Uncle Jimmy, Auntie Olive and Grandad Edwin.

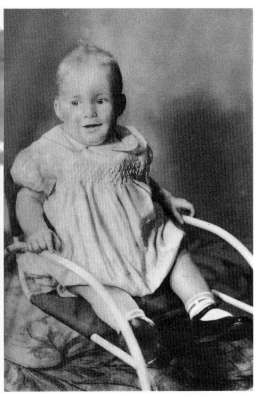

I always wanted to be a fireman!

I was pretty fashion conscious even in those days! The quintet (from the left) is cousin Carol, yours truly, sister Lynn, cousin Keith and brother Barrie. I think someone got the date wrong!

(ABOVE) Me at fifteen in Hatchers. I can't remember who lent me the jacket and tie!

(LEFT) My Welsh waistcoat and well-padded – with all 15 stone of me.

(ABOVE) Guess who's won – after the presentation at the final of the 1979 World Championship. (*Sheffield Newspapers*)

(RIGHT) Home with the cup – and I still can't believe it! I didn't even have time to go to the hairdresser's that day.

(ABOVE) The Silver Fox and I without our 'red coats' at Butlins in 1979.

(ABOVE) The banners say it all.

(BELOW) Dad and Peter Francis dressed to kill.

Never forget your Welsh.

WELSH BITTER.

(TOP) One of the strangest one-piece cues I've ever played with.
(ABOVE LEFT) On Tis-Wos with Isla St Clair. My hair's never looked so good!
(ABOVE RIGHT) Three very special dogs – Darren, Wayne and Goldie.

OPPOSITE PAGE
A dream come true for Wayne and myself – a visit to Anfield and our hands on the European Cup with the then captain Graeme Souness. We had a wonderful day out and met all the Liverpool team. The way we were looked after proved to me that this was one of the world's greatest clubs – both on and off the field.
(Harry Ormesher)

(TOP) My first luxury home in Pembrey, January 1980. Being world champion made it all possible.

(ABOVE) An unlikely team of parents line up for the team photo before a match against their sons at Llanerch Fields. I'm in the back row, second from the right, and Annette (front row, far right) is really set for the fray.

That victory over Alex was followed by another, this time against Bill Werbeniuk. After a scrappy start, I really settled into my rhythm and took the match 9–3, making 84 and 119 breaks in the last two frames.

So here I was, in another important final, against John Virgo. But curiously I could not get myself suitably worked up about it. Obviously I wanted to win the title; it was very important for my reputation as the new professional and world champion that I did. But by the time I had started to play a bit, John was 7–1 ahead. Although I did pull back to 7–5, by the end of the day's play John had an 11–7 advantage.

The final day got off to a quite bizarre start. The afternoon sessions had begun at 1.45pm throughout the tournament. But to fit in with BBC Grandstand's coverage of the final, Saturday's session had been put forward to midday. John had not checked the revised timetable and was resting in his hotel 15 miles away when the phone rang. He raced over in the car, got stuck in traffic and ran the last few hundred yards to the Guildhall. By the time he arrived, half-an-hour had been lost and, according to the rules, he had to forfeit two frames.

In the meantime I was sitting there not knowing what was happening. As far as I was concerned, I had virtually lost the tournament. I was not playing that well and John was too good for me. When they told me he would have to forfeit those frames, I just did not want it to happen. I thought they were pinching the championship away from him. When we eventually started, naturally enough he could not pot a ball. By the interval I had won both frames played and so levelled the score at 11–11.

Now I felt awful. John had gone mentally. It was going to be his first major championship win and now it was being stolen from him. That's how I felt about it as well. So during the interval I went into his dressing room and said, 'I'm very sorry about this, John. I don't know what to do.' He was pretty upset. 'It's nothing to do with you. It's not your fault.' So I said, 'Well, do you want to share the prize money?' There was a pause, then he snapped back, 'But you haven't won yet.' Of course, he was absolutely right. All it was was a gesture on my part. I had not assumed I was going to win, but really by then I was odds-on. Interestingly that conversation, I am sure, spurred John on.

The crux of it was that after the interval I went 13–12 in front, needing one more frame. All of a sudden I did not know if I wanted to win. I had a lot of criticism over this afterwards, particularly from the people who had gambled on me. Those who knew me realised what had happened. I was 13–12 up and I was going to win – no doubt about it. I was not going to try to lose. I did not have it in me to do that. But in the next two frames I just went for every shot, some of which I would normally have played safe, and lost both to give John victory by 14–13.

When they presented him with the cup, I thought: Well, it's right. He's won and he should have won. Losing those frames was unfair on him and the result had come out right. I was happy the way it had turned out. Being an afternoon finish, I had arranged to play a match against Tony Meo that evening at the Potters Club in Manchester. I played out of my skin and won 5–2, which showed that the UK result had not had any effect on me, which it would have done if I had lost the final under normal circumstances.

People accused me of not trying, which was unfair to John because I did try. Without those two frames I think he would have won easily and I still believe I did the right thing there. Whatever anyone else thought, it was right for me. I knew somehow I would win the UK eventually and when I did, in 1982, it gave me a lot of satisfaction. Things have a strange habit of turning out that way sometimes.

When the next event came round – the Woodpecker Welsh Professional Championship at Ebbw Vale Leisure Centre – I realised I had not played serious competitive snooker since November. What with exhibitions all over the country and moving into our new house in Pembrey, I had been fully occupied and so was really looking forward to the tournament. I reached the semi-final, where I had to play Doug Mountjoy, but it did not turn out to be a particularly happy match.

We had each won a frame when the referee called for an interval. I could not believe it. We had only played two games. Apparently it was to fit in with the television schedule, which on a normal occasion I would have willingly agreed to. But this was a national championship. After some discussion, it was decided that we would play on. But by now I had lost my concentration. As it was, I should have taken the break to settle myself down again. By the end of the session I was 5–3 down and never made up the ground afterwards. Doug won 9–6 and went on to beat Ray Reardon by the same score in the final to take the title.

I soon got over this disappointment with the Benson and Hedges

Masters at Wembley Conference Centre. I played well to beat a curiously careless Cliff Thorburn and then white-washed John Spencer 5–0 in the semi-final, finishing off with a century break. This meant another final appearance against guess who . . . yes, my old adversary Alex.

Now I had been playing some of my best snooker ever at Wembley and was confident of beating him again. By the end of the afternoon session we were level at four frames each, when Alex came up to me and asked if I wanted to do a deal on the prize money. In this case, it really did not matter because we both wanted to win. I agreed and that is what happened. Ironically, Alex only won one more frame as I took the Masters title 9–5 with a final clearance of 131. I know a lot of people would say I was wrong to have done it, but it did not make any difference to me. I wanted to win the tournament. The following year, when again I played Alex in the final and we were very much in the same position at the interval, he did not ask me to share the money. And when I mentioned this to him later, he said, 'Oh, I fancied beating you that day.'

Well, I learnt a lesson there. I had fancied beating him the previous year, but that did not come into it. Obviously Alex did it then because he thought he was going to lose. Then I realised how Alex looked at it compared to me. Nowadays that sort of thing does not happen – or very rarely.

I went on to complete a Benson and Hedges Masters 'double' by winning the Irish version in Dublin, which proved more interesting for the controversy I stirred up than the snooker itself. It all arose from the fact that both the Masters – the English and the Irish – were invitation tournaments. I had already brought up the question of tournament guarantees for the world champion with the WPBSA and it had been put on the agenda for the next meeting. In the meantime the organisers came over to invite me to play in Dublin. I told them that because these Masters were invitation events, the world champion should always have a financial guarantee. It was not just for me. I felt it should be automatic every year – and for all invitation events. The matter was brought up subsequently at a WPBSA meeting but kicked out.

In the meantime, I had to make a decision as to whether I wanted to play or not. I decided I would, but by this stage my relationship with the sponsors was not what it might have been. I felt I was going there to play under a cloud.

Kevin Norton, who works for Benson and Hedges over in Ireland and who has become a very good friend since, told me later that he was walking up the stairs at the tournament venue – Goff's – when one of the lads there asked, 'What's the score?'

'It was 10–9,' he replied.

'Who's won it then – Doug Mountjoy?'

'No,' he said, 'that other bastard's won it.' We laugh about it now, but at the time they obviously misunderstood what I was saying. They thought I was trying to squeeze them for money, which was not what it was about, really. I just felt the world champion should automatically be on a guarantee for invitation events.

Kevin and I are now very good friends and he comes over and stays each year on a short golfing holiday. He always pulls my leg about that incident when we meet. 'Don't forget the fish and chips in 1978, Griff!' Of course, he is referring to the time before I won the world title and had no money!

With the World Championship now looming again, I was starting to suffer the old malaise, homesickness, badly. And as a result, I began having a rough time both on and off the table. On the table I was involved in a new tournament, the British Gold Cup at the Assembly Rooms in Derby. We were grouped in fours, with each playing three frames against the other three in the group. Alex – again! – was in my group and needed to beat me 3–0 to go through. He put in a fantastic performance that day with clearances in all the frames – first a 46, then a 135 and a 134. Needless to say, he went on to beat Ray Reardon in the final. I then went to Ipswich for the Tolly Cobbold, which was being covered by Anglia Television. I had by now lost my form completely and made a hasty exit from that.

Off the table, the situation was even worse. When I came home for a day between engagements, the boys would ask me when I was going off again. I was starting to break up with it. I was seeing little of Annette either. The few days I was home I had loads of mail to see to and then I was off again on the road. I was also having some bad nights away in hotels and feeling very lonely and depressed. The effects of the year's events were finally catching up with me. Miraculously my snooker had not really suffered until now, which looking back was difficult to understand.

Shortly before the 1980 World Championship got underway, I had Dennis Taylor down for a few nights of exhibitions, one of which was at the local club in Cross Hands, just up the road from Llanelli. With my title defence at stake, BBC Wales wanted to do an interview, so I arranged with Peter Walker to conduct it at the stage door of the hall, partly because I knew we would be on a tight schedule and also that there would be less people hanging around there for autographs. In fact there were about a dozen or so kids there. Although I did not realise it at the time, I was in a terrible state mentally.

I did the interview and then the kids there wanted autographs. By now I was panicking about the match, which was already running late. So I mentioned to Dennis that we would have to slip in quickly before any more kids caught us for autographs. Then this woman, who was obviously one of the boys' granny, said quietly, 'Aren't you proud that the kids have asked for your autograph?' Well, that just did me in and tears came to my eyes. It had hit me like a ton of bricks because I knew she was right and I was wrong. I could feel myself filling up and I said to Dennis, 'Quick, let's get inside.' Dennis realised that I was in a bit of a bad way, although I was trying not to show him that. We went in. Up until that time I had been playing for months in front of the public, happily mixing with the crowds and chatting and signing autographs. Now suddenly everyone was getting to me. It was really heavy. Of course it was an accumulation of the last nine months and I could not handle it anymore.

The match finished and I remember all I wanted to do was to go round and sign autographs for everyone there to make up for what had happened earlier. It made me realise how important your public image and things like autograph signings really are . . . and how lucky I was that people asked for them. Really I had had a breakdown and did not realise it.

At this time I could feel I was going against the game that had been so good to me and I loved so much. It was hurting me. One day I arrived home having been on the road for about two weeks. I went in and saw Annette and she made me a cup of tea. Then I went straight into the snooker-room and had a knock on the table. And I realised then that it had nothing to do with the game: it was just everything that surrounded the game. That helped me a lot. I still loved playing, although I had had a belly full on the road. You see, the playing side was so little compared to the travelling and meeting people. They probably took up something like eighty per cent of the time. Annette did not really know too much about what was happening to me then. And I tried not to show her these things because I knew it was hard enough for her as it was – being known as just Terry Griffiths' wife and losing her own identity. And obviously the kids were getting similar reactions at school. Now they were no longer Wayne and Darren anymore – they were Terry Griffiths' sons.

Looking back overall, of course I enjoyed my championship year. There were disasters as well as triumphs, but the experience I gained in those twelve months was more than I have gained in the other forty years of my life, because so much happened to me. But the lasting impression I will always have is that it dragged me away from my family – and that is where my base was and always will be.

So it was under a general cloud of depression that I went up to Sheffield to defend my title. I had deliberately kept bookings to a minimum in the weeks running up to the championship to give myself time to prepare both mentally and on the table. But I could not ease the tension I was under. And this time it was all so different. Now I had everything to lose and nothing to gain.

I had drawn Steve Davis in the first round proper. As champion I was seeded straight into the last sixteen. What irony! There was the man who was to become my main rival on the snooker table and playing in the tournament from a position very similar to my own the previous year – relatively unknown and drawn against an established player, but with every chance of winning. And so it proved.

Strangely enough I was very relaxed when the match started and remained so, even though I found myself seven frames down. I did not even start to panic when I was trailing 10–3 and in fact at the end of the second day had pulled back to just 10–6 down. At 10–10 in the next session I was back in the match, but as Steve told me afterwards, all it did was to take the pressure off him. I had to agree. He won the last three frames, including a 116 break, and my title had gone.

Steve went out to Alex in the quarter-final and eventually Cliff Thorburn took over my crown. Naturally I was disappointed, particularly when it really sunk in a few days later. But, as I said at one interview after the game, 'It's not the end of the world. It's just the end of the World Championship for me this year.' Unfortunately that has remained the case so far ever since, although I came within striking distance in 1988, when I lost in the final to . . . yes, you know who.

As the dust settled on the season, Annette and I gave a lot of thought to moving away. One reason for this was that it would enable me to spend more time at home because I would not have to travel so far. Annette talked about it at length because she had had enough of it all. This was not helped by the fact that when I came home after being beaten by Steve in the first round of the World Championship, rumours started to spread about Annette. Friends told her that there was talk in the town about my losing. People were saying 'What can you expect with what's happening with his wife?' They were saying she had left home. She never left home. She never has left home.

It took us a few months to hear about this, but it had been going round for a while that Annette had left home before the championship with I don't know how many snooker players – and one was Dennis Taylor, whom we had become very friendly with by then. Annette and Pat, his wife, used to come round the circuit with us, which wives had never done much before.

We were staying with Dennis and Pat at the time, when a News of the World reporter appeared at the front door. He was a bit taken aback when I opened it. Having got over the surprise, he said, 'I hope you don't mind me asking, but we've heard your wife has left home and come up here to live with Dennis.' So I just smiled and said, 'Well, she's here. Why don't you ask her?' Unfortunately by now the national press had got hold of the story. It was worse for Annette, because everytime she went into Llanelli, people were talking behind her back. She found all the gossip very difficult to take and understandably thought seriously about moving away. But I never really wanted to move. My home was here. All my roots were here. And so too, of course, were Annette's. So we decided eventually to stick it out – and now with the new club and house we have put our roots down even deeper.

11 For Snooker's Sake

I MAY HAVE many failings as a person and a snooker player, but lack of commitment is not one of them. Whatever I get involved in, I always try to put total effort into it. The main problem with this is finding the time and the energy to sustain this commitment. And so I found out with the WPBSA, particularly after I was elected vice-chairman.

Following my success in the World Championship in 1979, as I have already mentioned, I played a much more active part in the work of the sport's governing body and people listened to, and I hope respected, my views on all the important issues that were discussed. That year had proved a very hectic one for me, but I still managed to find the time to spend on what I regarded as vitally important matters that affected not only the game but, as a result, all the players involved with it.

During that first year, one of the burning issues was the system of voting, which on paper was highly democratic. All registered professionals had an equal say in the organisation and running of the sport. But that meant that the top players, who numbered very few, could be and were often out-voted by the rest. And that never struck me as being a particularly reasonable or sensible situation. After all, without those top players, you would not have prestigious tournaments, extensive television coverage or major sponsors. And these were now proving to be the life blood of snooker.

The situation came to a head after that Sheffield final in 1979 when a number of WPBSA members decided it was time to break away and set up a rival organisation which was to be called the PSA. My agent Del Simmons was heavily involved in these moves and, as a member of the ISA team, I felt I should go along with the idea and support him. I certainly agreed with the principle that the top players should have more of a say in where the game was going, although I did not want to deny the other players the right to have their say as well.

When I was not playing or travelling between venues, for about four months I was constantly on the phone talking to WPBSA members who either wanted my support or my opinions on what was happening. Although I understood and agreed with the idea in principle, I did not know anymore about it than that. Having never been involved in the political side of snooker before, I now found myself right in the thick of it. My dilemma was that I still had a lot of time for the WPBSA, which had run the sport for many years, but I also sympathised with what the PSA was trying to achieve.

As things turned out, the PSA never really got off the ground as a rival organisation, partly because the WPBSA did decide to alter its constitution to go some way to meeting these criticisms. So the big split never took place. Nor sadly did the hoped for improvement in the game, as the WPBSA continued to control all the snooker tournaments.

But there was, as far as I was concerned, a much more important point at issue here – and that was the basic qualification requirement to become a professional player. And over the years it changed so much that in the end nobody really knew where they were. And certainly during my years on the board it was a major regret of mine that a final, workable solution to the problem was not found.

I believed then – and still do – that the right professional qualifications were the most important part of the game. At one time you had to be either the English or World Amateur Champion to be accepted into the professional ranks. So the chances of joining were very limited. But it did ensure that only the best got in. That was the rule in 1978 when I applied. This was then changed to allow anyone who had represented his country at international level to apply for professional status. Later, it seemed, as long as you were well behaved and well dressed, you were taken in. It was the same old thing. People who did not understand fully were complaining about a closed-shop situation and the WPBSA was succumbing to this criticism, particularly from the press. I believe we should have been much stronger and stood firm on this issue.

Out of the 128 professionals now playing the game, in my opinion at least half of those should not have been allowed in, for a variety of reasons. My attitude has always been the same about professional status. When I joined the ranks in 1978, I was very proud to become professional. I had become part of a well-run set-up with very high standards. Over the years all that has changed.

There are now a lot of people playing snooker professionally who still work part-time as well – club managers, for example. And really most of them are not up to the standard. You only have to look at results. I cannot see how you can possibly have players in the game for so many years who never move out of the bottom ten or twelve places because they never win any matches. All they are doing is taking the places of young players with considerably more potential, who because of the system have been prevented from joining in their place.

Fortunately this is at last changing. We now have ranking tournaments each year, which are not ideal but at least it does bring in the playing side, where the man who performs best on the table gets the chance of becoming professional. But it was not always the case and that was one of the major regrets I had when I was on the board.

Another problem the game suffers from is that over the last few years I have noticed so many players who do not dress properly, who spend most of their time in the sponsor's lounge drinking and often do not know how to behave. In short, they do not project the right image for a professional snooker player. I feel embarrassed when I see some of them. When you go to these tournaments where there are 64 qualifying players, it is like a bloody circus. Many spend their time in the players' room after free drinks. They are never playing; they are just hanging about. I really do not understand what they are doing there. I find it very sad to see what has happened over the last few years. I believe the WPBSA should take action to control this by only letting in the very best amateurs. If you have not got the necessary quality, then 128 is definitely too many. I am all for giving any player a chance, but on the table. If he proves to be good enough, then he should be allowed to compete professionally.

People tend to forget how different the professional world is to the amateur game. It is a business – and it is tough. You only have to look at the number of young players who have come into the game in recent years and see how few have actually made it in the big time. Jimmy White turned professional in 1980 and has of course gone on to establish himself as one of the game's greatest attractions. Other than him, there has been Neal Foulds, John Parrott and, most recently, Stephen Hendry. But that is a total of just four who have made the grade over the last eight or nine years.

When people say, 'Give the young players a chance', they do not seem to realise how hard it is going to be and what little chance they have got of making it. And how good they are as amateurs does not really come into it. When they become professional, it is a totally different world. There are loads of players who turn professional. It is just that they have not made the grade and, in my opinion, it will always be the same. Even if you had 500 professionals, only a few would make it.

One of the problems, I believe, is that young people generally find it difficult to adapt to the professional game. I do not mean the playing side; of course they can do that. But snooker, like any other sport, is not only about playing. You get one or two good results and the press are all over you. They are at your door, getting you to make statements, taking photographs – and all of a sudden you have been put in a position you know nothing about. The next time you go and play, your mind is all over the place. You are not a snooker player anymore; you are a personality. And most players these days cannot handle it because they have not got the character, and so it affects their game. They have not gone through a long apprenticeship by playing in the amateur game for ten or twelve years and using it to form their character. As a result, they are exposed and vulnerable.

On top of all that, it is bloody tough playing against the best in the world, whatever the sport. It is bad enough for established players; think what it must be like for beginners. Nowadays youngsters serve a very short apprenticeship and go into a full-time job as a professional as soon as they can. From the start they must compete against the very best. It takes most people a long time to settle into this kind of situation and very few make it, as has been proved. And it will never be any different.

Snooker has reached the stage now where there are a lot of young amateurs who mature quickly on the table; but that is all. If they win and get exposure on television, then they think they have moved forwards. To an extent that is true and they are obviously happy with that. And three or four years later they are still happy with it. But to make the grade – to win a major tournament – how many are going to do it? Stephen Hendry has, but he is really the only one. It is very difficult for them and I do not think it is ever going to change.

Certainly the younger players who have come into the game over the last few years are more professional. They present themselves well, perform well and behave well, even if they are not making it on the table. And I like to see the game projected that way. Part of the reason for this is that they are better managed. But that is to do with money, of course. Because there is more money, so there are more managers. Nowadays everyone seems to have a manager. It may be their best mate; it does not matter. But what is the manager doing there? Is he advising him? Is he criticising him? Is he giving any help apart possibly from putting some money behind him? I do not think so. I am sure there have been more players breaking up with managers than making the grade.

Young people have come up and asked me for advice and when I have given it to them, they have ignored it. So, if a young player is not doing well, what does he need a manager for? The manager cannot do anything for him. He cannot get him work or exposure, until he betters himself on the table. When he has done that, achieved something and got a name, then he needs a manager. Often you hear them say, 'I'll have to get sponsorship.' But how can they get sponsorship if they have got nothing to offer? Possibly they may make the grade one day, so what they are really asking for is a loan, with no guaranteed return.

Looking back at my younger days as a player, the amateur game was a tremendous training ground for any aspiring professional. But it is not the same anymore. Now it is a semi-professional game in its own right. To me, the amateur game now is what goes on in my own club in Llanelli. It is about local players, local leagues and competitions where people compete for the honour of winning. When you talk about the national amateur game now, there is not one. All people are doing is playing for tournament prize money. None of them work anymore. Instead they travel around the country each week; they are all full-time players. Once upon a time the English Amateur Championship was the biggest event of the year. Now it is just another tournament with a different name. The amateur game as I knew it has gone – and again it is all down to money.

I try to keep up my links with the 'amateur' game in Wales as best I can. But all they seem to talk about now is the money. When I chat to the players, it is not about the black they missed or the fun of the game anymore. Instead they talk about the £500 they could win for a tournament and the fact that they had to go up there four times to play!

Obviously the game has improved on a general level because more people are playing than ever before. But that in itself creates a problem, because you do not get the stars anymore. None of them are good enough to go out ahead of the others and on to professional status. A new player comes along and he goes professional as soon as he can. So the game keeps losing players at the grass roots. You find little sense of love for the amateur game now.

Loads of youngsters I have spoken to have said that if there was no chance of going professional, they would pack in the game. So they are just playing snooker to go professional, not playing for snooker's sake. I would be the first to admit that there is nothing wrong in having ambition. But you also have to be realistic, since very few will finally make it. But they all think they have a chance and who am I to say otherwise? Stephen Hendry is a perfect example. His amateur record did nothing to suggest he would become a top professional in such a short time. But he came out and proved it on the table.

The trouble is you cannot give them all a chance. The game is getting swamped with preliminary rounds, with something like 60 amateurs playing off to get into a professional tournament. There is even talk now of a secondary professional system; but we are still talking about amateurs. They do not seem to understand. They are saying that there are 96 professionals and there should be a promotion and relegation system to decide the rest – including amateurs. That is like Liverpool saying, 'There is a team in Llanelli that plays football as well. Don't you think we ought to give them a chance to play in the First Division?' It strikes me as crazy, but they just do not seem to look at it that way.

I can never understand what the objective is in all this. The game's authorities are not looking after the people they have got in the pot now. So what are they talking about looking after other people for? They say it is for the advancement of the sport. But where is it? Even if they had 5000 snooker players, there would still only be the few who made any money and the public wanted to see. Every player has got to prove he can make the break-through and become a top player. Until he does that, he does not count. I know it sounds cruel and nasty, but it is true.

I have always felt very strongly about this and made my point even when I was on the WPBSA. Eventually I resigned, but it was not over this matter specifically, but mainly on the Pot Black situation.

I instigated the move either to turn Pot Black into a proper tournament with prize money or get rid of it. It did get the game off the ground on television, but there was a lot of wheeling and dealing going on. People were being invited to play for commercial reasons who should not have been there. And the money the WPBSA was accepting from the BBC at the time was scandalous. While sponsors were having to pay £100,000 for a tournament, Pot Black was giving us a pitiful £10,000. There were also favours being handed out under the table and I tried to expose this. On top of it all, the series took up sixteen weeks of our television time, which was particularly precious to us when we were trying to attract new sponsors.

I put up with the situation until 1982. For two years the board had said that if Pot Black did not come up with the right money, it would stop it altogether. But each time it went ahead. The crunch came when I joined up with Barry Hearn (that's another story!). Barry had got involved because Steve Davis had just signed up a massive endorsement for Pot Black snooker tables with Leisure Industries.

'What difference does it make to you if Pot Black continues?' Barry said to me one day.

'Because I think it's wrong,' I told him.

Barry was of course looking after Steve's interests as his manager, but not mine – and we were beginning to fall out about it. In my mind the situation was quite simple. Either I stayed on the board and tried to get decisions taken against my manager's interests or I came off it.

Just before I resigned, a few people who had previously suppor-ted the idea that Pot Black had to go changed sides when it came to voting. And I found out afterwards that a few favours had been done for people on the board. I could not and would not compete in that sort of world. It was totally alien to me. I was not a businessman, just a snooker player. I was not used to politics and I did not want to be any part of what was going on. I also saw a danger in the possibility that Barry might try to influence decisions on the board through me and I did not want to be compromised. I certainly had no intention of falling out with Barry, so I thought it was best if I resigned.

I was chased by the press afterwards, particularly since I had also turned down the job of chairman. I had refused that because I did not think I was qualified. I had never openly criticised the board outside our meetings and generally still feel that most of the people on it were doing the best they could under the circumstances. The problem was they were just the wrong men. The game had moved on too quickly, there was too much money involved and it had got beyond my scope – and others, too. Unfortunately I was one of the few to realise that and come away. Others have stayed on for the wrong reasons and, in my opinion, that is why the game has not advanced as it should. For a period of four or five years snooker enjoyed a tremendous boost in popularity, but the board did not go with it. There were too many narrow-minded views. And all this was taking up too much of the very limited time I had which I needed to spend on my game and with my family. But the Pot Black incident really finished it for me.

Ironically Pot Black did eventually die a death. In the end they all saw the light. But there was no way it could go on. We were just making fools of our sponsors and that we could never afford to do. Sponsors have done so much in recent years for the game, although it has not always been for the good.

Certainly the Eighties have proved a very exciting time for snooker and I would be lying if I said I did not enjoy being part of it – seeing the game grow to a stage where there are now millions of pounds of prize money every year. To say that we do not want the money would be stupid. But when money becomes involved, it creates problems – as with the board and the question of discipline and of course all the publicity it attracts.

It is not so much a question of the game changing, but more of how it has changed. I have no doubt in my mind that the best years of my life were when I played amateur snooker. I used to love the game and met a lot of nice people in the process. You would shake hands after you lost. The disappointment was still there, of course, but that was it. There was no money involved. Over the years that relationship with other players has changed – through the money, through the competitiveness, through the pressures of a weekly circuit we never used to have. Before, there were just one or two main tournaments a year. You could develop friendships when you were on tour or in exhibitions. Now there is a major championship every few weeks and with each you get the bitterness, the back-stabbing . . . they are all there now and I think it will only get worse.

I know I have taken money out of the game. I would not deny it. I have enjoyed what it has given me in my life. But it has ruined professional snooker for me. Now it is all about the money. I have said in television interviews that the money does not mean anything. And it does not when I go out to compete. But a ranking tournament would not mean anything if it was only worth £500. At the end of the day, everyone wants to get into the position where they can earn the money. At the moment there are probably only half a dozen players earning really big money. So the other 122 all want to be the 6.

You cannot tell me that all they want to do is win a tournament. If they had the choice of making money or winning tournaments, they would take the money . . . unless they are liars – or just very rich people. When someone says at the end of the season, 'I'm Number 2 in the rankings', what he really means is 'I've earned £500,000'. For me, the money has taken away a lot of the enjoyment.

Television dictates sponsorship, so television has over the years had a lot to say in the running of our game. Again it is down to money. If television says it wants the best of nine and the board does not agree, then there is no television and no money. And so in its own way it has ruined the game as well. Everyone wants a slice of the cake. But as the slices get bigger and bigger, they also get fewer and fewer. For several years I have thought there has been too much snooker on television. Even when I was on the board, we were very aware of it. But it was difficult to turn down a tournament for £100,000 because there are those who need the money and the competition. The trouble is we no longer leave our audiences wanting more, which I think is the secret. I also believe the game should be taken round the country more, so that the public at large get a chance to watch snooker live and not just on television.

(TOP) Snowbound in 1982 for the Lada Classic in Oldham. I was picked up by helicopter but had to leave my two young supporters behind.

(ABOVE) Don't we look sheik – if a little under-dressed – in Dubai!

(*Daily Mirror/Monte Fresco*)

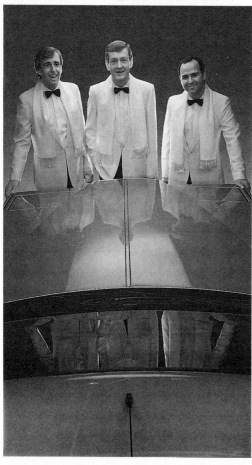

(LEFT) 'Remember the fish and chips?' Kevin Norton with Dad and myself in Goff's during an Irish Benson and Hedges. Whoever called me 'big mouth'? (*Frank Fennell*)

(BELOW) Me and my German friends in 1986.

(BOTTOM) Barry, with his fan club, looks set for a marathon along the Great Wall of China during the Matchroom's 1987 Far East Tour.

(ABOVE) The perfect follow-through. Did I really make it to the 18th this time?

OPPOSITE PAGE
A Goya Matchroom after-shave photo session with the original team – now all major individual trophy winners! (*Frank Tewkesbury/The Standard*)

(BELOW) This is what life to me is really all about – at home with the family.

(TOP) The 'Dubliners' relaxing during a Benson and Hedges tournament. In case you don't recognize the hairstyles, there's (from the left) Steve, Del Simmons, me, Kevin Norton, John Virgo and Cliff Thorburn.

(ABOVE) Ball-crusher Ganley, who's become a very good friend of mine on the circuit.

OPPOSITE PAGE

(ABOVE) On a trip to Dallas, with two of my best mates.

(BELOW LEFT) The original team reflected in the bonnet of a £66,000 Aston Martin, which only one of us could afford at the time – guess who!

(BELOW RIGHT) Beauty and the beast! Guess which? Me and my FJ 1100 Yamaha.

(RIGHT) I'd prefer to go hungry, but the strange eating habits of the Chinese have no effect on Neal's appetite.

(BELOW) At last! A plane trip without my cue. Annette and I on holiday in Las Palmas.

(BOTTOM) Our two best friends – Alun and Heather – with us on holiday at Disneyworld.

(TOP) The matchroom at my club – my pride and joy. It's amazing to think that this was once the first revolving stage in Wales, part of the Glen Ballroom. (*Ron Bevan Photography*)

(ABOVE) A double dream come true – first the club and then my new home, reward for ten years in the professional game. Not bad for a postman!

12 The Big Decision

SINCE 1982 MY snooker life has been all about my life with Barry Hearn and Matchroom. And although, looking back, I never regret having made the decision to join up, at the time it was probably the hardest thing I have ever had to do.

I had been under contract to CSS for two years, during which time Barrie Gill had just handled the commercial side of the business. I was still coping with all the day-to-day affairs such as fixing engagements and booking hotels. But it was reaching the stage where things were getting too much. With more and more tournaments and other appearances, I really needed someone to look after my arrangements on a daily basis. CSS was never going to offer me that; it had never been the intention.

I did think of opening a local office, employing a secretary and running the business that way, because then I would still have total control over myself and my work, which I did enjoy doing. It was just all the paperwork that was really getting me down. When I did get home for a few days, as I have already mentioned, I was writing letters, answering letters, going through the mail and then going away again. It was putting a lot more strain on my married life than it should have. So in the end I decided to look for a manager.

There were a few companies involved in snooker management by then. I went to see Richard Town, who had a set-up near Stoke-on-Trent. He sounded very impressive and had lots of thoughts about what he would like to do. So I was seriously toying with the idea when, almost out of the blue, Barry Hearn came along. This would be around May 1982. At the time he was just looking after Steve Davis and Tony Meo. Now in those days I suppose Steve and I were one and two in the world. We were playing each other regularly and fought out several important finals. Certainly on the table he was my main 'enemy'. I really had not given Barry a thought, simply because I did not think he would be interested in taking on any other players.

When he found out I was looking for a manager, he gave me a call. 'What's this I hear you're looking for a manager? Why didn't you give me a ring?' It took me by surprise because while I had a good relationship with Barry, Steve and Tony, it just had not entered my mind to go with them. But we had a few meetings and discussed things. From my point of view, up till then I had had almost total control of my life. Now Barry did not want to come in just as a day-to-day manager. He wanted to take over my life completely. And this, I thought, would be a very severe blow to my freedom and independence. It meant that everything would be taken away from me and put in the trust of another man, whom I did not know that well, although to be fair I had total trust in Barry from the early days. I thought it would be fine if he did all my bookings for me. But he said he did not work like that. 'You either come with me or you don't.' I respected his point, but it made me think a lot more about joining him and so I delayed my decision.

For his part, Barry could not understand why I was hesitating. We would have these meetings, usually in hotels which were the normal places for this sort of thing when you were on the circuit, and Barry would go through all the things he could do for me. Of course he really did not have to sell himself to me because his ability to manage was by now well-known. And I remember him saying to me one day as we were going through a whole load of things, 'I can't understand why the hell I'm doing this. Why am I trying to sell myself to you? I'm the best there is and that's all there is to it. If you don't want to join me, don't.'

Not knowing Barry as I do now, I said, 'That isn't the point. I want to join you, but it just seems such a major step to give everything up.' Because everything would go through Barry, my accounts, my cheques, all my banking and the personal appearances, and all of a sudden it seemed as though my whole life was going to be taken away from me. So I had to give it a lot of thought.

Being the type of person I am, what I do in those circumstances is to go round asking different people their opinions. I have always been very open about asking people if I want to know things. But everyone I asked in snooker said the same thing, 'Don't join up with Barry Hearn.' It stuck in my mind more than anything else, because these were people whose opinions I had always respected. They told me that if I joined up with Barry I would always be number two next to Steve Davis. I could understand their point. But I looked at things as they stood at the time and I was number two to Steve, whether I joined Barry or not.

After my defeat in the 1980 World Championship, Steve had knocked me out of that year's Coral UK Championship in the semi-final with a 9–0 whitewash. He again ended my hopes of a second world title in 1981, when he beat me 13–9 in the quarter-final and scored another victory later that year in the semi-final of the Northern Ireland Classic. I was then on the receiving end of an emphatic win in the 1981 Coral UK Championship, when Steve won 16–3 to retain his title. Success came at last early in 1982 when I beat him 9–8 in the final of the Lada Classic and then 9–5 to win the Benson and Hedges Irish Masters. In between he had got the better of me in two other finals – the Benson and Hedges Masters and the Yamaha International Masters.

My record with Steve was there for all to see and so I respected everyone's views on this. It meant a lot of heart-searching and, of course, many discussions with Annette. Again it was my upbringing and coming from Wales . . . and now I had to consider sending everything up to London. If I make a decision, then it is always 100 per cent. I never do anything by halves. It was the same when I decided to turn professional. So I wanted to be as sure as possible in my own mind.

But I cannot stress enough how difficult a decision it was. The problem was not joining up with Barry, but losing my independence. Annette was not totally for it, but at the same time she knew I needed someone to do my work. It was a matter of making the right decision at the right time. I discussed it over and over with her and finally she said, 'You've got to do it. You're the one that's involved. You've got to make the decision, it's up to you.' She was never actually against me signing with Barry, but she shared the same reservations as I. But once the decision was made, Annette accepted it and did not get involved anymore.

It all came to a head when I was at the Cliffs Pavilion in Southend that June, playing in a tournament Barry was promoting. Prior to

109

that I had been speaking about it to Ted Corbett, the snooker correspondent for the Daily Star. I wanted his advice and spoke 'off the record'. I really opened myself out as to the dilemma I was in and the trouble I was having coming to a decision. Ted in his wisdom went away and wrote a story for the paper that I was not going to join Barry.

Now I had promised Barry I would give him an answer at Southend, which then was about two weeks away. So you can imagine how angry and upset I was when I read the article. I immediately picked up the phone and rang Barry, because obviously he had seen the piece and read that I was not joining him. He was very good about it and told me not to worry. Of course he realised what had happened, but it had put us both in an unpleasant position.

I did not see Ted again until the first tournament of the new season, which was in Derby. I can see him now walking towards me in the Assembly Rooms and he realised what he was going to get. I told him in a few short words what I thought of him and what he had done. I had had an incident with Ted before when he had put something in the press that I did not think was right and I had told him so then. Of course, they have a job to do and can report what they like. But when you tell them something in confidence, you expect them to honour that trust, especially with the snooker boys who become part of the team and are with you week in and week out. Anyway, it was the second time with Ted and as far as I was concerned he was finished. I just stood there, looked him straight in the eye and told him what I thought of him and his principles. The man went right down in my estimation because he had pulled that stroke.

When I arrived in Southend, I was still very much undecided. But the moment I saw Barry, I made up my mind. I walked straight up to him and said, 'I'm in,' and shook his hand – after all those weeks of indecision. 'Great,' he said. 'Let's go and sign the contract.' So we sat down, Barry pulled out the contract and I signed it. It was the standard contract – Barry took everything I ever owned . . . and I have said yes to everything ever since!

That was in June.

All of a sudden I did not have any paperwork anymore and then I realised how much time I had been spending on it. It was wonderful.

I had so much time on my hands. Of course the snooker carried on as normal, but apart from that I had so much time to spare and it felt strange, because I had been so busy over the last three or four years. It really hit home to me then how important it was to have a good manager on a day-to-day basis. There was, of course, the hiccup with the WPBSA, which I have already mentioned, when I felt I had to resign from the board. But that cleared the way for us to establish what has proved to be, on the whole, a very happy and successful relationship.

So I started the 1982/83 season with my greatest rival on the table as a partner off it. And what a battle we had together. Our first confrontation as team-mates was in November, when we met in the quarter-final of the Coral UK Championship. Just to confound my critics, I beat Steve 9–6 to avenge my 16–3 thrashing in the previous year's final and went on to beat Tony Meo, my other team-mate, in the semi-final. I think, however, I did put a smile back on Barry's face by winning the championship after another tremendous match with Alex Higgins.

Barry, of course, was now in the middle. In those days he came to a lot of the matches and used to join us in the intervals, because he was totally involved in the management side. And I remember thinking how difficult it was for him with Steve in one dressing room and me in the other. Steve was obviously his number one – and always will be. But I had knocked Steve out and then Tony.

When it came to the final, of course Barry was 100 per cent behind me. He told me afterwards how amazed he was at the way I handled it. He could not understand how relaxed I was in between games and sessions and commented on how much difference there was between me and Steve. Steve really gets himself psyched up and if he has a very bad session he shows it afterwards. Barry realised then what an easy-going person I was. I have always taken things very much as they come. I was laughing and joking and actually singing when I went out to play; and that is what I enjoyed. I used to relax before I played and that helped my playing.

That night Barry laid on a big champagne celebration for me. I must have appeared very ungrateful because having spent a decent amount of time saying hello to everyone and accepting the accolades, I retired to bed with Annette while the party continued without me into the early hours. Barry's only comment was, 'Good

God, here's this party going on and Griffiths has gone to bed with a cup of tea!'

After that final in Preston, I had to go straight to Cleethorpes to play Steve again in an exhibition and from there down to the World Doubles Championship at Crystal Palace in London to partner Doug Mountjoy. This was not an itinerary I would have chosen for myself. I would have given myself a break between tournaments. After winning the UK, I badly wanted to go home. Apart from winning it and wanting to go home and share my success with family and friends, which was always very important for me, I wanted a rest from the circuit and time to repack my bags. After all, I had been away about three weeks. But I could not do it and it was then that it dawned on me that Barry was going to book me too many shows if I did not watch out. So I decided we had to get together and have a chat about it.

I remember leaving Preston and saying goodbye to Annette, who had been up with me during the championship. She was going home down the M6 and I was going up the M61 to Cleethorpes. I so much wanted to go home with her. I could feel the emotions of the championship coming out of me and we had a few tears before we parted. I just did not want to go to Cleethorpes.

I then went down to London for the World Doubles and Doug and I got through to the final. This was the first year of the tournament, at Crystal Palace in London, so that was another opportunity lost since I always used to get a break during that competition. We lost to Steve and Tony in the final and afterwards Barry came into the dressing-room. This was my chance to tell him how I felt and I was in the right mood for it.

'There's no way you can book me up like you book Steve,' I said. 'I'm a man who likes his home life and I must have breaks between tournaments so that I can play at my best, which is the most important thing.' I think Barry got the message.

Naturally Barry would accept as much work as possible if he thought I would do it, which he did. But there is a balance between different people. Tony at the time was not getting a great deal of work, while Steve was in great demand and working every day of the week; and Barry thought he would get me as much work as he could, too. I had to explain that it was not what I wanted. If I went on the road more, I would earn less because I would be losing more tournaments. I can remember the look on his face when I told him that. I could see he did not like it. But it had to be said. He was not used to his players confronting him.

Barry looked on me slightly differently from the other two, anyway. Steve was his best mate, Tony was very young and needed guidance and now he had a man who had joined him as an established name in the game, who had had success and who was also very much his own boss, and the same age, more or less. I think he realised the relationship was going to be different. After that, Barry still tried to get as much work as possible, but he did space it out more – and we never spoke about it again. With Barry, once you say something, that is it.

There are, of course, times when you have to have long spells on the road because matches and dates just fit in that way. To be fair to Barry, he has always tried since then to work itineraries in as best as he can. By this time the game was booming, there was a lot of work about and naturally he did not want to miss any of it.

I have never, for one minute, regretted joining Barry and still do not – seven years later. Lots of people told me I had made a mistake, but that was their opinion. From my point of view, at that stage in 1982 I was thirty-five. I did not know snooker was going to take off as it has now. It was obviously very popular and becoming increasingly so, but you never know what is round the corner. So obviously from a financial point of view I knew I would be far better off joining a team like Barry's.

My respect for Steve off the table was also a major part of my decision, because I thought if I went with Barry we would have a good team and I knew at least Steve would be one of the top players for many years to come, without possibly realising he was to dominate the game in quite the way he has. It was a big decision in my life, one of the biggest I have ever made, and I know I got it right.

But it was not easy to start with. I had always been very friendly with other players, promoters and officials – I got on with every-body, really. Then, when I signed with Barry, I noticed a few doors had closed in my face. People were not so friendly anymore. I noticed straight away that the reaction people had to Barry and Steve was being applied to me as well.

Barry and Steve were not liked very much within snooker circles.

Steve, obviously, was not very well liked because of his success and, to be fair, because of the way he was. He was with Barry so much and tended to be off-ish with the other players. That was his choice and it probably would not have mattered if he had not been so successful. But he was and the players disliked him.

Now I found I was getting a different reaction. Those who used to phone me up and tell me about the inside politics never rang anymore. They all changed. I was still the same person, though. I may have got a different manager, but I had not changed at all. But others looked at me differently. You could feel it in the players' room, where if you lost there were a lot of happy faces. These were the same faces that a few months before would have been disappointed for you. Perhaps 'disappointed' is the wrong word. They did not really care. But now they did care. If you lost, they would think: Oh good, Barry Hearn's lot. He's joined them – he's one of them now. It became a crazy situation and, of course, it has carried on.

Barry has been very heavily involved in the advancement of snooker over the years and has come under strong criticism from all different quarters. In my opinion, he has had very little recognition from the right sources within the game for what he has done for it. He has never had the recognition he deserves, mainly because of his outspoken views. He upsets people very quickly through being like that. But it is also because of Steve. Everybody hates a success story, I am afraid, unless they are involved in it. I got involved in it, became part of it and to begin with found it very difficult to accept the narrow-minded attitudes with which I was now confronted.

By showing true team spirit we rode the storm. And we were a team – Steve, Tony, myself and Barry. It was never just the three players, always the four of us. And over the next two or three years I found things happening just as I thought they would. Barry more or less cut my work load by half and doubled my wages. So how could anyone in those circumstances turn round and say: 'I don't think he is good for you'? It is not a matter of opinion; the facts are the facts. Barry delivered the goods – and lots of them. He started organising endorsements on a team, rather than individual, basis. He had been doing a lot with Steve but now we were doing things together. We went on our first tour abroad – to Thailand, Hong Kong and Kuala Lumpur. They were very happy days.

If I got knocked out of a tournament I would give anything for

Steve or Tony to win and they felt the same. We were a team, there is no doubt about it. We wanted each other to do well. We knitted in well together. Tony was the lowest ranked player of the three, Steve was the most successful by far and I slotted in the middle – more established, with a good image, the older father figure in the team. It was a good blend and we all mixed and worked together like a family.

Then, in 1984, Barry built the new matchroom club in Romford and decided to call us Matchroom. Although I did not realise it at the time, this was to prove very significant. Things were starting to change. Plans were afoot and within a year events were going to create a major and, for me, unfortunate upheaval that was to destroy our 'team' for ever. Equally significant, I was beginning to go through a crisis of my own making – on the snooker table itself.

13 Crisis with the Cue

I HAVE ALWAYS enjoyed the involvement of coaching and trying to help others develop and improve their game. I was very pleased when, after my season as world champion, Billiards & Snooker Wales offered me a contract to go round its eight snooker clubs and hold coaching classes for the members during the summer months. It was a good PR exercise for the company, since it got a lot of publicity and even local television coverage. Certainly to my knowledge it was the first time a professional player had done something like that on such a scale.

But for all the success it achieved as a company promotion, from the coaching side sadly I did not feel it worked out. With some of the clubs I went into there were 150–200 people, with whom I had just two hours to spend. It was impossible. They were divided up on different tables and I went round each one in turn. But I could only spend a few seconds with each and therefore was unable to offer much practical advice. Of course, it boosted club membership at the right time and I was pleased for the company. After all, it was costing them money for me to be there.

From a positive point of view, it did get me involved in coaching and from that I started to show a lot more interest in the technical side of the game, particularly cue action, which I had never really bothered that much about before. Since then I have coached a lot of good players at home and in some cases offered advice to fellow professionals where I could. I love coaching. For me, it is as good as playing and I certainly get as much pleasure out of it.

One of the pupils to give me particular satisfaction was Tony Chappel, a local lad and a very promising player, who fulfilled his potential by achieving professional status. So far he has not done as well on the circuit as I thought he might, although he did beat Steve Davis in the Mercantile Credit Classic at Blackpool this year. But at least he is there and has every chance. I also coached a young lady called Sian Newberry, from Neath. She was for a while one of the leading women players in the country, although sadly she has recently lost a bit of interest in the game.

One of the few things I really enjoyed when we toured the Far East for the first year or two was to take any coaching sessions that were arranged. Although any of the players could have done it, none of them really wanted to and it was left to me.

I remember on one occasion we were in the Queen Elizabeth Stadium in Hong Kong and the organiser of the coaching session had told me to expect about 200 or 300 people. I was a little taken aback when 1200 turned up! So there I was, standing in the middle of this mass with a chap called Joseph translating for me, and I had to try and give a coaching session to 1200 Hong Kong people. It was absolutely tremendous and just showed what interest there was in snooker over there. In fact there were more people who turned up for coaching than came to watch the tournament the night before. It was over-whelming. They just kept coming in.

The trouble with coaching, however, is that really it has to be done individually. Groups are difficult to teach effectively, whatever the numbers! But that makes it a very time-consuming job. More and more youngsters now come to me for coaching, particularly now I have my own club, but sadly I just do not have the time to spend with them all, as much as I would love to.

My growing interest in coaching naturally involved me in a much deeper analysis of the techniques of snooker and by 1982 I was beginning to look more closely at my own game. This period coincided with a string of defeats at the hands of Steve Davis and that set me thinking. Was I going to accept the situation as it was, where I was having great difficulty beating Steve, or was I going to try to better myself and improve my technique?

Having joined up with Barry, as I said, I found I had a lot more time on my hands. Basically Barry was doing all the work and I was just playing snooker and would spend many hours on the table by myself, experimenting with my technique – different grips, different stances, different ways of striking the ball – all in a effort to improve my game. I have to admit that eventually I got too hooked up in it all.

117

Around this time I packed up smoking and went on a keep-fit programme. I had never attempted anything like this before, but was determined to make the effort. The month before, I planned to go on a diet – no sweets, cakes or sugar – because I knew I would put on weight when I stopped smoking. I spent much of the first week in the garden to keep myself occupied and after two weeks had lost a stone. It was a desperately hard thing to do, but once I felt I had kicked the habit the satisfaction was tremendous.

I chose the summer because the tournament pressure was off and I had time to get myself in good shape. I even read a book or two on psychology and started to dabble in the art of meditation. I was having some lessons in yoga with a friend of mine, Gwyn.

Each morning I would get up early and go running down in the forest just below the house in Pembrey. Then I would come back and do some exercises. But I found all that too much of a strain. After a year and a half I was not smoking and continually watching my weight and I just could not settle down and relax in my spare time. I packed it all in. It was really starting to get me down. I was dreading getting up in the morning and was becoming a very unhappy person. I even started smoking again because I thought it was affecting my play, which of course it was not. That was one of the worst decisions of my life. And for that first week every cigarette I picked up I hated, particularly after all the effort I had taken to pack it in in the first place.

During this period, the only way I could relax at home was on the snooker table. I could not watch television like I used to because I would just sit there and eat and I was putting on too much weight. So I spent crazy hours on the table. I was playing eight or ten hours a day by myself. How much good this did me is certainly open to question. The problem was I did not then have the technical knowledge and, for various reasons, did not get anyone to help me with it. But I carried on like this for a couple of years. Every time I went into a tournament, I was using a different technique. It was not working, but I never lost my belief in what I was trying to do. I was having a few good results and a lot of bad ones, but that did not really prove anything. I was going backwards, although I always believed I would eventually turn the tables and go in the right direction.

The grip was the first thing I worked on and I tried no end of different variations. I would put hundreds of hours into practising each one. Then I would try it in a major tournament and then, maybe months later, decide it was was not working out and try something different. I found I was getting so heavily involved in this side of the game that the playing side was taking second place. When I went out to play, my mind was on technique and not on competing. And when this demanded 100 per cent concentration, I was not able to give it. My mind was on other things and my performances dropped right down as a result.

I got plenty of reaction from others – professional players and friends – asking, 'What the hell are you doing it for? You were good enough before.' But I kept saying I was not good enough because I could not beat Steve. The trouble was now I could not beat a lot of other people I used to beat before, either. But I strongly believed I would find a way.

I must have tried about twenty different types of grip with the fingers, closing the hand on the cue at different times . . . and every one took months. Then I tried to move my body about, to realign the shot to go with the different grips and ways of my hand hitting my chest instead of dropping my top arm going through. Once you have tried different basic things, then there are hundreds of permutations within those. I also experimented with the eyes – when to bring them up to the object ball, which you must do in snooker. There are quite a few different times you can do that, I can tell you. I would then bring that into my game and try it for a few months, I was turning myself into a technical freak, there was no doubt about it. But, in a curiously perverse sort of way, I had never enjoyed myself so much practising. Now I had an incentive to go and play all the time.

I was certainly changing as a player. I was much more knowledge-able technically – and much worse on the table. The way I looked at it was that I had had a lot of success and won a lot of tournaments. I enjoyed that but I had to look somewhere else to keep my interests going. My basic game has always been sound enough to keep me up with the top players. In that respect, my instinct to compete had kept me at a certain level. But I was now no longer winning tournaments – even smaller ones. But I gave myself plenty of time and kept telling myself: You've got to be patient and it'll come.

The turning point came late in 1985, when I was up in Preston for the Coral UK Championship. I decided to go and see Frank Callan. Now Frank is a very knowledgeable person when it comes to snooker. He has coached a lot of the top players, including Steve, John Parrott and, more recently, Doug Mountjoy. My problem was that Frank was based in Preston and I was in Llanelli, about five hours' drive away. So I could not see him regularly.

At the time, Frank was working quite a lot on Steve's game and since I was playing Steve a lot in tournaments, I asked him if he minded my approaching Frank for some advice. He had no objection and Frank was only too pleased to help. So now I had someone with the knowledge to help sort me out. Together we went through what I had learnt over the last few years of trial and error – mostly error – and tried to knit everything together. It worked very well, because Frank saw things that I could not have spotted myself. If only I had gone to him in 1982, I would not have had to struggle for so long over my technique. It was not an easy thing to admit, but it was true.

Because I had been world champion and a big name in snooker, I reckoned I knew all about the technical side. The truth is that very few players know anything about it. And why should they if they have got the natural talent to play well? But that is the other trouble with me. I am such a perfectionist, particularly when it comes to snooker. My friends have always told me that it is one of my biggest failings. I was never just happy doing something. I wanted to know why I was doing it – and why I was not doing it. I kept striving to try and find the answer. At the end of the day we are all human and we have good days and bad days. In 1982 when I was good, I was very good. But sometimes I was bad; it happens to everyone. I just had the feeling I could get myself up to a higher level when I was bad. I was not worried about my best game. I did not think I could improve on that. But I wanted to improve on the bad days, hopefully to get through to the next round when I might play better.

Frank had studied my game – he watches everyone's – and told me what he thought about it. I tried a few things out and they worked very well. The trouble was I would not see Frank again for another three or four months. If I could have spent more time with him over those few years, I would have improved my game a lot. Frank is great company because he loves to talk about the game, the matches, the technique of different players. I really enjoy discussing snooker with him. And I have learnt a lot from him on the technical side and picked up a lot that I do not think anyone else could have shown me.

Frank works very much to a method and would always preach a method to me. That was helpful because I can be very sloppy in my own way and I lose any method I have very quickly. He would stress the importance of doing the same things every day and I got into the habit of making a list of all the things we had talked about and I would keep referring back to it. He would stress the importance of catching the centre of the cue ball and I would tell myself: You're not doing that today. No wonder you're playing badly. His method definitely works. He also used to get me in the right mood to play. He had that knack of psyching me up before a match, which was also important.

A lot of fellow players could not understand why I spent time with Frank. 'What do you want a coach for when you can play the game to such a high standard anyway?' It is a problem for those who are obviously blessed with ability. When they are playing badly, they want advice, but they also want to remain natural – and you cannot have it both ways. I want to know why I am playing badly. So I went to Frank to look at the technical side and find a way of playing better. But I must be honest, six years later and I still have not found a way. I have found ways of playing better, but they do not work consistently. Natural instinct is really the most important thing, together with a good mental attitude. I find when I am feeling good and really psyched up, I play well. So what has that got to do with technique?

I have not been going to see Frank quite so much in the past year or so. One problem is that Frank and I used to disagree over certain aspects of technique. He would have one opinion and I would have another. Being the type of people we are, I did not want to waste my time or his going over things that I did not believe in. There were, for example, things he wanted me to do with my cue action that I was not totally for. He wanted me to have a very long cue action, whereas I wanted to try it shorter. There was no point in my going there and getting advice and then not sticking to it. If you do not believe in your coach, then you are wasting your time and his. But overall Frank has been a great help – and a very good friend.

Certainly I do feel there has been a positive side to this period in which I analysed technique so closely. It may not have brought me instant success on the table, but it has convinced me of the importance of good coaching, which is something I would love to do if and when I ever decide to give up playing. It is one of my ambitions in life to set up an advanced coaching school, with the right facilities and hopefully the right knowledge that I have obtained over the years. I do not know all there is to know about cue action, for example, but I

121

think I know as much as anybody, simply through trying it out myself – and in the heat of competition, which is the most important thing.

I have found over the years I have developed my technique that in practice I was unbeatable. It was phenomenal. I just was not missing at all. Days and days went by when I was playing out of my skin. But the following day I would go into a match and it was not working, because all of a sudden there were other things that needed my immediate attention, which I could not give them because my mind was fixed solely on technique. In practice you are much more relaxed. So I found in competition so many of the techniques that worked well in practice were falling apart. I had not experienced this before because my old technique used to stand up under pressure. It may have been good or bad on a particular day, but at least it would not change. I lost that edge, that aggression I used to play with, because my mind was concentrating solely on the technical side. For amateur players wanting to improve, this is the best thing you could ever do. But I certainly do not advise it for top professionals.

It has probably taken up the major part of my time over the last few years, when really I should have been thinking: I'm playing Steve Davis tomorrow. That – and that alone – should have been on my mind. And I have never really been in a position to settle into one technique and put my total concentration into the competition. Considering that, I have done remarkably well, in my opinion. I have even managed to adjust in the middle of a match, which normally I would not recommend to anyone. In the last year or two I have brought more consistency into my game and am getting into more quarter and semi-finals. There have, of course, been other pressures on me recently, but generally I am feeling a lot happier with my game and am confident the results will not be long coming again.

14 Matchroom: For Better, For Worse

IT WAS THE summer of 1985 when Barry Hearn signed Dennis Taylor after he won the World Championship. And I, for one, was not particularly happy about it. We had been together as a team for three years and during that time had established a very good relationship. It was like a family. But now a fourth player had been adopted and I realised things could never be the same again.

From a professional point of view, I accept that the game was changing. We needed more players and at the time Dennis was the obvious choice. Now I had known Dennis for many years and my complaint was not against him personally. But Barry had always said that if any major decisions had to be made, we would all get together and discuss it first. That never happened. Really Barry went ahead with that on his own.

It would be wrong to say I was opposed to Dennis joining us. It was the way it happened that I objected to. The first thing I really knew about it was at a press conference Barry had arranged at The Brewery in East London, at which it was announced that Dennis was joining the team. That annoyed me and I think Steve and Tony felt the same way about it as I did.

This was the first time the team had changed in three years. It meant we now had a four-man set-up. Of course, Dennis is a very good professional and was definitely going to be a valuable addition. Apart, obviously, from the playing side of the game, where we now had three world champions, Dennis had always been very professional off the table, as well. So it was not as though we thought there was anything wrong with the choice of player. The point was we did not know whether we wanted any more players. If the three of us had been involved in the discussions, we would probably have decided

123

against it. But looking back on it now, it was really Barry's decision and we had to stand by it. Dennis had won the World Championship, beating Steve in that pulsating final, where the result hung on the very last black, and for him joining Barry was obviously the right decision.

Unfortunately things got off to a bad start when we went on our Far East Tour, the first time we had gone with a fourth playing member of the team. It also proved to be the first time we had any waves within the team. We arrived in Singapore and almost immediately there was a disagreement between Dennis and myself over the format of the tournament. Every time we had been out there to play before, we had adopted an aggregate points system to decide who went through in the event of two players finishing with the same number of wins from the 'round robin' section. I did not agree with it, but this is what the organisers of the tournament had decided and we went along with it. Anyway, Dennis beat me 2–0. But because I had potted the colours to keep up my points tally, while he had not really tried on them, I ended up the winner on aggregate.

So now there was a dispute. And it was not very pleasant, to say the least. It was not that Dennis wanted to stamp his authority on the team, but I think he wanted to make sure we were not going to take advantage of him. Not that we would ever have considered doing that anyway.

We were all sitting in the hotel lounge while it was decided who had qualified. Steve was already through and, as far as I was concerned, so was I. It all got very heavy and Dennis went over to see the organisers. Meanwhile Steve and Tony did not want to know. It was difficult for them to support me, because it would then put Dennis out on his own. But they both knew what had happened. And we did not like to make it too obvious, particularly with the press there. The last thing I wanted was any kind of scene. I would rather have gone to bed and let them carry on. But I decided to stay and see what happened.

The organisers made their decision – I was in the final. Dennis took it quite badly and made a few comments out of place. And now, from being a very happy team all those years, suddenly Dennis had come in and stirred up a hornet's nest. I felt very upset about it, not just the incident, because those things happen, but the fact that Dennis had come into the team and we had got a problem in the very first tournament we played together.

Barry was at home through all this. When we rang him, he told us it was up to the organisers to sort out what they thought best. Dennis was very upset because he thought he was in the right. Meanwhile I went into the final in totally the wrong mood. It had caused a lot of unrest among the team. We had just started the tour and had three weeks ahead of us. There are enough problems anyway, what with being overseas in a strange country, with all the travelling, and I for one certainly did not want this kind of aggravation as well.

We then went to Thailand. Now Steve had been the first player there in the early days and to the locals he was *the* player. There was a big reception at the airport when we arrived, with cameras flashing away and girls waiting to put garlands of flowers over our heads. Of course they all went straight to Steve. Dennis was the world champion but they did not see it that way in Thailand. To them, it would always be Steve. He was their number one. So Dennis, who was visibly upset, turned round and said, 'Well, who's the world champion here?'

Never before had we had anything like this, because we had always accepted things as they were. Of course we all knew and accepted that Dennis was the world champion. Steve was not trying to up-stage him in any way. But I could see that Dennis felt he should have been having all this treatment and Steve should have been in the background. I think we all felt then that this was wrong and started to regret Dennis joining us. While he was normally very professional both on and off the table and had an excellent public image, to be fair it was a very difficult situation for him. But I felt he should have handled it better.

So now, for the first time, we already had unrest in the Matchroom team, and Barry would not get involved. 'Don't be so bloody daft. It'll sort itself out,' he said. Of course it did. It had to for everyone's sake. But it was not easy.

I have known Dennis, as I said, for quite some time. Our wives had become very friendly and we used to visit each other's homes. So I decided I would have to pick a suitable moment to sort it all out with him. Steve could not do it; he was not the sort of person to sit down and have a heart-to-heart with anyone. Nor could Tony. It was down to me. And for the good of the team knitting together, I felt I had to say something. There was definitely friction, which I would put down to several things. We were all individual people. Dennis was champion of the world for the first time in his long career and he had

125

worked very hard to get where he was. Now he had achieved that success and all of a sudden he was not getting the number one treatment. I think, deep down, that was what the trouble really was. And I cannot blame him for that.

The opportunity came when we were all in Australia. It was the last thing in the world I really wanted to do, but I felt somebody had to take Dennis to one side and thrash out what was going wrong. To be fair to Dennis, he listened to me and then talked through it. It was not an easy thing to do – for me or him. Normally I do not care what I tell people; I am very open in my views. But I did find it difficult in this situation. The last thing I wanted to do was to hurt or upset Dennis. Apart from the fact that we knew each other well, we also had to play each other on the table. To give him credit, he took it well and accepted what I said. And I am sure it cleared the air a lot.

Of course, after Dennis joined us, it was only a matter of time before more players followed. Willie Thorne was next. He arrived in March 1986 and within a few months Neal Foulds was also with us. So now, all of a sudden, as far as I was concerned everything had changed. The close-knit relationship we had developed had gone. Dennis, Willie and Neal were good lads, but you were talking about three different individuals. We were now trying to make it into a six-man team, which was impossible to do. To try to get six individual players together, when they were all fighting each other on the table, was just not on. Matchroom was now well and truly formed. The word 'team' had, in my view, become obsolete a long time ago.

Interestingly, since we had given Barry so much stick over Dennis joining, we had all discussed beforehand the arrival of Willie and Neal. But the pressure had been building up for some time, particularly over the Far East Tour, which Barry realised he could no longer fulfil with just four of us. He needed more players to do all the shows we had. To begin with, he had to go outside the Matchroom to get other players, but it was now his ambition to have enough of his own. And this he finally achieved when first Jimmy White and then Cliff Thorburn signed up. Now Matchroom was eight strong, with some of the best players in the game.

Apart from the effect all this had from a player's point of view, there was another significant consequence, which hit me just as deeply. In the early days we had struck up a very personal relationship with Barry. He was at the other end of a phone any time of the day or night, always there to give help or advice. But as the others joined, Barry started drifting away from us. With so many players, you just cannot keep up that sort of contact with all of them. You would be on the phone all day and all night if you did.

To be fair, Barry is still on the end of a phone if you have problems. That is one thing about him, apart from the professional side; there is never a problem that Barry will not listen to and try to help you with. He will always do anything he can.

But when he takes you over, it works both ways, because he really does help in other respects. For example, when I joined Barry, I was trying to sort out some of my old contracts that were still flying about, He got totally involved in what was an awkward situation for him. Also, when I have had bad press, particularly in the early days when there were the stories about Annette going off with other players, Barry was helpful and very supportive.

In a way, he has become my best friend on the snooker circuit. Although there is a great distance between us physically, we have bonded a very close friendship. I do not see Barry that often now, but it is nice to know he is always there if anything happens.

The Matchroom is now a tremendous success story, there is no doubt about that. It has swept the world with snooker. But if you ask me about Matchroom as a team, then it has not been a success. It finished when Dennis joined – and then the others. The whole thing changed. When we go on tour, of course, all the boys get on well; they are all good company. But it is not a team anymore, not what I would call a team. There are just too many of us. You have got eight different characters with different temperaments and really they do not knit together. Also you have got the bitterness and the jealousy of defeat by your team-mates. But that is bound to happen. I think a defeat from a fellow Matchroom player hurts more than a defeat from an outside player. It is very tough when we meet in competitions, because we do not like losing against each other. And although the boys are very professional when they lose, it does hurt and they tend to stay away from each other for a day to two.

But snooker was growing at this time. We had to grow – and in a way Matchroom has grown out of all proportion. Now it is probably as well known as the Liverpool football team. Everybody has heard of Matchroom. That was Barry's aim and he has achieved it, as he normally does, with a few hiccups along the way.

But do not get me wrong. There have been a lot of positive and enjoyable aspects of being part of Matchroom that I would not have missed for the world. Much of it has been very exciting, like being the first players to go to Thailand and Singapore to promote the game. And we have been involved in some crazy things along the way. I remember Steve and I doing an ad for one of our sponsors – Kan Win of Hong Kong. We shot it in a house in Hampstead and then they dubbed it in Chinese. It was hilarious and they actually showed it on BBC's Sportsnight one week.

There have been a lot of endorsements, including one with Goya for men's cosmetics. That was a first for snooker. Now Barry always treats these things very seriously and we had to visit the factory where they explained how each perfume was created, what all the substances were and why it was so expensive! It was quite fascinating, really. After all that we had to select the perfume we wanted for our endorsement. Then store visits were arranged all over the country and we spent a couple of hours in each signing autographs. There was a lot of publicity before each event announcing which player was coming and we would go round with a microphone asking people if they would like to try some Goya Matchroom. It was all so exciting, so different.

We also had a big deal with Rileys – a team contract – which involved events in snooker arcades and large stores such as those in London's Oxford Street.

One particular Goya promotion sticks firmly in my mind since I got myself involved in a rather farcical situation with a very good friend and travelling companion Gareth Owen. After the family, Gareth has certainly been my biggest supporter and has followed me all over the country, tournament after tournament, win or lose, since 1983. Not only that, but he has had to bear the brunt of my cue power on the table at the Mario Berni's Mackworth Club in Neath for literally hundreds of hours.

On this occasion I was due at a big Leeds store to help sell the Matchroom cosmetics and Gareth and I had decided to make a detour via Blackpool the day before to watch some of the World Amateur matches that were taking place. I remember we were watching a very exciting game between Gary Kwok and an Australian which ran on late. I insisted on staying till the bitter end, even though we were due to book in at an hotel in Leeds that night.

When the match was over – it finished 4–3 – we went to the multi-storey car park to collect my car. To my horror, when we got there the place was locked up for the night. So I could not get the car out and, worse still, we could not rescue our bags either. So we stayed in Blackpool without any luggage and had to collect the car in the morning, from where we had a bit of a dash to get to the store in Leeds on time, grabbing a wash and a shave on the way.

Poor old Gareth always seems to get involved with my mishaps. One time he had to run a rescue mission from Llanelli to Warrington after I had turned up for the Mercantile Credit Classic with no dress shirts. While I was waiting for him to bring mine from home, I had to borrow some off John Williams, the referee, which were several sizes too big for me. All in all, 1984 proved a pretty hectic year for Gareth, but I am pleased to say he has stuck with it and I am always grateful for his friendship and support.

After being an out-and-out snooker player, I was getting involved in all sorts of promotional activities – and, of course, seeing parts of the world I had previously only dreamed about. Strangely at the time the significance of it all did not really register. But when I look back on it, this was the first time snooker players had gone to countries like China and Japan and we were acting as pioneers for the sport. I felt very proud about that. And the way we were looked after was tremendous. We were treated like royalty.

Barry has always insisted that if we do not travel first class, we do not go. His view was that if we set ourselves up as the best in snooker, then we should always project that image. This did create an unfortunate situation a few years ago when we were invited out to Australia by Eddie Charlton to play snooker. We turned it down because we were not given first class travel. There was a lot of bad publicity over that, although as often happens not all the facts came out. Barry had offered to pay the difference betwen the fares. The trouble was that Eddie had arranged a cheap rate with the airline for a block booking of tickets and did not want to advertise the fact, which he would have had to do if Barry made up the balance.

Although incidents like that did tend to give us a bad image, overall it has been very good, mainly through our success. And we have managed to keep this going. Generally we have dominated tournaments and without doubt our most successful season so far on the snooker table was in 1986/87, when Matchroom players between

129

them won every major tournament. So when one of us lost, it was making headlines. The press could not wait to knock us down if we did not win. But that is the same for anyone who is successful in sport. You create a very big image and sometimes you forget how big it is.

Having said all that, things are not always as rosy as they seem. Are they ever? In our case, something I have noticed is that there are times when players will not make sacrifices for the good of the team. And that is why I have said that it is not a team anymore. One example is the golf day we hold every year in Chelmsford for the lads from the Romford Matchroom Club as a 'thank you' for all their support for the players, some of whom do not bother to turn up. It may not seem important to them, but it is very important for the club members. Unfortunately there are quite a few things like that.

One of my present roles in life is acting as spokesman for the players when there is anything involved with the Matchroom that needs to be discussed. Normally it is down to me to get things going and I try to get the boys together to find out what their views are. This probably stems from the fact that I speak my mind and am not afraid to tell other people what I think. Also, as the oldest player of the group, I am the one they all talk to when there are things they do not want to tell Barry about themselves. Unfortunately it has always been on an individual basis; they never seem to stand up and support each other. I have tried in some cases to get them to make a joint decision, but it has never happened. As far as I am concerned, it has got to be everyone together or not at all. And really I do not think we will ever see the day when that happens. Having said that, even if all eight of us did ever agree on a decision and Barry said no, that would be the end of it.

A perfect example of the team not pulling together happened in 1988 when there was an unfortunate incident involving Rothmans which created a lot of ill feeling and bad publicity. The company had sponsored a Matchroom League around the country and a new contract for more money had been virtually agreed. Apparently at a late date Rothmans pulled out and Barry, who was understandably pretty upset about it, threatened legal action.

In the meantime the Rothmans Grand Prix, which was a world ranking event, was due to take place – in October. Because of the situation that existed between us, Barry decided that we should not recognise the sponsors and refuse to do any interviews or associated publicity for them.

I felt this was not the right thing to do. As far as I could see, we had four options. We could drop out of the tournament completely, although with ranking points at stake this would prove very unpopular with the players. We could play, but give any prize money to charity. We could do as Barry eventually decided. Or we could carry on as though nothing had happened.

I took it upon myself to speak to the other players about it. Steve agreed with me that the best course of action was to take part but give any earnings away to charity. But the whole team had to do it and nobody else agreed. To me this highlighted the problem of Matchroom. The players would do anything together until it affected their pockets. One or two of the players even said: 'It's alright for you two; you've got plenty of money. But we're broke.' This attitude really upset me.

Barry was very upset too. Had everyone stuck together, the protest would have been a lot more effective and Matchroom would have come out with a much better image. As it was, we did not do any interviews or attend press conferences and as a result – quite rightly, in my opinion – we were slated for it. We were also fined £34,000 by the WPBSA. The amount of the fine was all about the rift between the WPBSA and Barry Hearn, of course, and no true reflection of what we had done. How can you compare our action with head-butting an official, for example?

As a footnote to all this, the irony was that Steve eventually won the tournament and would, on principle, have given up that £60,000. Even Steve would have noticed that!

Every business has its ups and downs, but taken as a whole it is difficult to fault such a success story as Matchroom undoubtedly is. In hindsight, it is easy to say that Barry should have done it this way, rather than that. But Barry is just so full of energy, he has got to be trying something new all the time. With some of the things he has tried, he has fallen flat on his face. But he is up straight away and on to something else. And that part of his character has been a tremendous help to me when things have not been going that well. If I have had a bad result in a tournament, Barry will come up and say, 'What's the matter? You're breathing, aren't

you? Go up to the cemetery and look at the people up there.' That is
Barry's outlook on life.

One thing you will never get off Barry is sympathy, because he is
very much a realist. Feelings and emotions have never been something he ever lets out. When you phone him after losing, he will say:
'You'd better pull your finger out and do better next time. Get some
practice in.' He admits he knows nothing about the playing side of
snooker. For him it is a case of winning or losing. There are no
excuses. You would never ring Barry up to explain how you lost,
because he really does not want to know. Either you are through to
the next round or you are out. It may seem a very cold approach, but
it is the only way to be in this game. There is no room for sentiment.
And if you have a manager who gets involved in the playing side, that
can be murder too.

I shall never forget when I lost to Vic Harris in the third round of
the Mercantile Credit Classic in 1986. Now Vic used to be with Barry
at Romford, but they fell out and Vic went his own way. He had just
come out of hospital to play in the tournament, so he was not feeling
particularly great at the time. Anyway he beat me 5–3 after I had been
leading 3–1. It was a very bad result for me and I was not feeling very
good about it.

So now I had to pick up the phone and tell Barry that I had lost to
Vic Harris, knowing from the earlier circumstances that they were
not the best of friends.

'Lost?' he said. 'What, to Vic Harris? But he should have been in
hospital. He could hardly walk.' And I waited for Barry to go in for
the kill.

'Well, Griff, what's another bad result in a string of bad results?'

I shall never forget that. It really just about summed up what had
happened. And I burst out laughing. It was such a funny thing to say.
Anybody else would have said, 'Oh well, we all get our off days.
There's always tomorrow.' Not Barry.

That incident really puts in a nutshell my relationship with Barry.
He completely sweeps aside the playing aspect and never says
anything about it. And when you consider it, after seven years, that
takes some doing. He will see you before a match and say, 'Come on,
you've got to get stuck in here and win this one.' But having said that,
he will not mention the snooker. If you play like an idiot and lose, you
know what to expect from Barry.

132

To highlight how important Barry has been to the game – and, more particularly, those fortunate enough to be involved with him – you only have at look at what is currently happening on the snooker circuit.

Last year when I was up in Blackpool playing in the Canadian qualifying tournament, it was like a circus; there is no other word for it. The matches were being played on no less than sixteen tables. People were hanging around playing cards and drink was flowing all over the place. When you went into the practice room, all you could see were wives, girl friends, families . . . and you are talking about somewhere players needed to use for serious practice for a major ranking tournament. I thought then: What the hell's the game coming to? Having come away from there, it was off to Dubai for a competition, then to France to play in the Norwich Union and finally back to Southend for the Matchroom Tournament. That was three prestige tournaments that none of the other players had. They were solely for the Matchroom. And the prize money available from those three was more than you could earn through the WPBSA in a year.

Suddenly you realise what sort of set-up we have got. Okay, if you do not win, then you do not get the big money. But Barry had always been of that opinion. You should play for the first prize: the best man wins and scoops the big money. All the players have got a guarantee, but the big money is only there at the top when you win. Winning is what it is all about. Barry has always said, 'If you win, you deserve the money. If you lose, don't come crying to me. You've had your chance to play in the tournament.' And that is an opportunity players outside the Matchroom never get. All they have are the official ranking tournaments.

The situation is perfectly summed up by looking at the annual prize money available. When this was published at the end of last season it stood out a mile. The list is broken down into ranking tournaments, those that are open to everyone and outside events, which are effectively Barry Hearn tournaments. Looking at the prize money in the last column compared to the others, you quickly realise how important it is to be part of Matchroom and how lucrative his tournament circuit is for the players involved. Barry has been heavily criticised for trying to split the game. But what he has done is to ensure that top class players get top class money. And what a lot of critics either fail to grasp or chose to ignore is that he is prepared to take risks to guarantee this. There have been occasions when Barry has had to support some of the tournaments financially because of the lack of sponsors. For example, the World Series fell through and Barry had to bale that out financially.

Criticism is not limited to outside Matchroom, either. There are sometimes dissenting voices from within. What I would say to those players is that they should consider themselves very lucky to be part of Matchroom and be happy with what they have got. It comes back to a point I made at the beginning. As far as I am concerned, the Matchroom team is Steve, Tony and myself. The other five are outsiders, and, to me, always will be. And I do not mean to be disrespectful to them. But they have been brought into the best snooker team in the world and are enjoying the icing on the cake. They should realise that. Without Barry and Matchroom, they would still be just one of the many WPBSA players – and not part of snooker's elite.

I feel very strongly about this and my feelings after the first Matchroom Tournament in Southend really say it all. The final was between Steve Davis and Willie Thorne, who had just joined us, and there was a £50,000 first prize for the winner. I remember watching the match and thinking: Steve's got to win this. He is the Matchroom. He was 9–7 in front, then Willie won the last three frames. And I sat there, saying to myself, 'This can't happen; this is wrong. How can Willie take money away from our team?' Of course I was totally wrong. Willie had joined us, he was part of Matchroom and he was entitled to win and take the money. But I still felt that tinge of disappointment. Not because it was Willie; it could have been anyone. But the money was going out of what I called – and still do – the Matchroom Team. Again, that is my narrow-minded Welsh opinion of things. But that is me, I am afraid, and I will never change.

15 A Club of My Own

EVER SINCE I turned professional, I had it in the back of my mind to own my own snooker club one day. And I thought it would be nice if this could be in my home town. I started thinking about it seriously early in 1986, but at the time there was nothing readily available or suitable in the area.

My elder son Wayne was now playing a lot of competitive snooker locally and I used to go and watch him play at Riley's in Llanelli as much as I could when I was home. This gave me a feel again for local snooker and the Llanelli League, which I was of course brought up with. I also followed my local team – Burry Port Legion – because a friend of mine Mike played for them and Chris, who now works for me in the club. Matches were on a Wednesday night and I thoroughly enjoyed this involvement with the local league again.

There is something about a local club that still grips me. There is a tremendous atmosphere in these places, with all the personalities, the players, the performances, the success and the failure, and I found I was getting more and more involved with it all. This led me to think seriously about having my own club and running it the way I wanted to – more for the snooker players than just a straight business proposition.

The problem was that with Riley's and the Pot Black Club, which had recently opened, there really was not room for a third club in the town. But then I heard that the Pot Black Club was up for sale. It was, in fact, Cyril Richards, my old friend who used to own the chain of Mackworth clubs I coached in some years before, who told me about it. He had had a look at the place, but due to some difficulties over the contract had not gone ahead. I was immediately interested and went to have a good look at the property. The building itself was in a pretty

135

poor state of repair and was obviously going to cost a lot of money to do up. So it was not, on the face of it, a great business proposition, but deep down I had a burning desire for a club and my heart was really sold on the idea.

It was in March 1987 that I got involved in the preliminary negotiations for the lease of the property. In the meantime, another building in Llanelli became vacant. That was the old Co-operative Stores in the main street. I looked seriously at that because it was a big building on an ideal site. The added attraction was that I could keep two shops there and the other two the council would take off me in return for a longer lease on my property. But deep down the Pot Black Club kept biting away at me. It had been the Glen Ballroom and before that the Ritz, where I had grown up and spent my youth. So there was a lot of nostalgia attached to the place for me. Mind you, it was really run-down. There was no proper heating. The tables were in a terrible state; the cloths were ripped and the cushions were off. And there was dampness everywhere. Yet it had an atmosphere. After all those years, I could still sense it when I went in the place.

So, against my better judgement, I left the Co-operative project, which was a much better business proposition, alone and decided to go for the Pot Black Club. Sentiment had got the better of me because of the special memories I had of the place.

The next move was to get Barry Hearn down to give me his opinion. With Barry's knowledge of snooker clubs over the years – he used to own the Lucania chain – it was important for him to see the club and tell me what he thought of it. So one Saturday morning he came down in his limousine with Robbo, his driver. I met him at my home in Pembrey and was greeted with the usual crack, 'We braked hard in Burry Port and still almost missed you.' After a cup of coffee, we got in the limousine and drove back to Llanelli to look at the club. Coming into the centre, we pulled up in traffic behind seven or eight cars and Barry piped up, 'Good God, just our luck. There's only eight cars in Llanelli and they would all be out this morning!'

We caused quite a stir when we pulled up outside the club, as you can imagine. Downstairs there is an amusement arcade and cafeteria and the bus station is right opposite. Everyone saw the limousine, which to be fair you could hardly miss. It is a great big ugly American job. And when something like that arrives in Llanelli, you can guarantee that by lunchtime the whole town knows about it.

I took Barry in and we went upstairs to the snooker club. He could not get over it. It was so ramshackled.

'What are those kids doing downstairs?' he asked me.

'They're waiting for it to open to come up and play.'

'What, you mean to say it's still open?'

He could not believe anyone would play in a place in that state. There were portable gas fires dotted around in a vain attempt to heat the club and the roof was leaking. So what with the heating and the water, you can imagine the dampness in there. I had had a survey done and knew that it would take a lot of money to bring the place up to scratch. But despite all that, Barry liked the club too and agreed it had the right atmosphere. So that was it. We decided to go ahead and buy it.

The necessary contracts were drawn up and by June the club was mine. Now I had to try and make something out of it all. The building was on three floors and I had the middle and top ones, although the top was an absolute wreck. Being the type of person I am, there was no halfway and I decided the only thing to do was to knock down everything inside – gut it completely, walls and all, and start again. So that summer, when I would normally be relaxing, spending time with the family and playing some golf, I had now committed myself to the club. I organised a small office upstairs in the old ballroom from where I ran the whole operation myself. I had decided I wanted to do it all, from helping to knock it all down to arranging the sub-contracting and hiring people. This meant I virtually lived in the place. I was there from about eight every morning until the same time each night – and sometimes a lot later.

For the first month or so I really enjoyed it. There was a small cafe called Dai's across the road which we used everyday. All the lads in Llanelli used to go there for a cup of tea and a sandwich and I found myself back with a lot of people I had been at school with, all working people I had been brought up with. This really brought me back to my roots again. To begin with they used to pull my leg every time I came in. 'Oh look,' they would say, 'here's Terry Griffiths coming in for a sausage sandwich.' It did not worry me and after a while they accepted me as one of them. It was a great feeling to meet them all and to work alongside them again. I was in overalls, knocking down walls, clearing away rubbish and generally mucking in. And with all the manual work, I never once thought about what it might do to my precious snooker hands! More than anything else I felt part of a team again, which I had not experienced for a long time. I was quite excited about it all.

There was a tremendous amount of work involved in knocking the place about. In total we filled something like 30 skips and eight massive lorry loads just with the junk we took out. We pulled everything down – all the walls, the ceilings, the lot. I say 'we', because I could never have done it without the help of my father, Wayne who came in right after school finished and a few friends like John, the window cleaner, and his friend Noel, and Chris, who as I have said now works in the club. They all came and helped out when they could. I had, of course, also paid a gang to come and do a lot of the demolition, but the other three used to come in after work and spend three or four hours sweating away. I did not have to tell them what to do. They just got stuck in and did it, since they had a lot more knowledge of this type of work than I did.

'Getting back down to earth' was really the wrong expression; it was below that. I was going back to my younger days and thoroughly enjoying it.

Amongst all the rubbish, you would not believe the amount of wood we got out of the place and I must have spent hours and hours sorting it all out and removing the nails. There were tons of the stuff. By the end, we had managed to pile timber up to the ceiling virtually across the full width of the ballroom. There was one hell of a mess for a while and it all incurred a lot of expense for me – and that was even before I started to put the place in some sort of shape.

There was a period then when Annette refused to come up to the club. I was getting so involved in it all, totally and utterly at this point; so much so that when Annette did appear I virtually ignored her. I did not mean to but I was just so involved. And even when the demolition was coming to an end and we got down to the construction work, it was the same. Because I did not have any knowledge of this part, I asked advice from people around and I used to get four or five quotations for every job that needed doing. There was a steady stream of people in and out, each one wanting to give a price. So I had to take each one round and show them what was involved, which in itself was a three- or four-hour job. Also, I was never off the phone. I had list after list in the office, with all the prices and other relevant information – and all this was so new to me. But it was a great challenge.

I seemed to be handling that part of the operation quite well, certainly better than the family, who should have had a lot more of my time and energy. With all that was going on I was forgetting about home, which in the summertime was what it should have been all about – with Annette and the boys. Inevitably Annette and I started to have a few quarrels. She was quite right, really. I had got too involved in it. So I tried to explain that it was our club, not just mine, and suggested she came and helped out. But I knew there was nothing she could have done before we had gutted the place and started putting it back together again.

One of the problems was Annette could not see any light at the end of the tunnel. Everytime she came up, it was an absolute shambles. We would get all this junk out one day and she would arrive the next and there was another load of junk. It just kept coming, because there were lots of small rooms to empty out and, since it had been an old ballroom, they had stored stuff everywhere. Up above the old stage, which was about 20ft by 60ft, the place was filled up with chairs. So when we went to get that ceiling down, there were more lorry loads to fill and it was like that in just about every room we went into.

The place used to be a single, complete unit, but over the years it had been renovated and converted into three floors – one for the bowling alley downstairs and a dance floor upstairs, with an apology for a restaurant on the third floor. When the upstairs was finally turned into a snooker club, all the existing junk was pushed into any available room or corner. And there it stayed until we came along and threw it all out.

As far as designing the club was concerned, I had asked a friend of mine, Keith Hughes, to draw up some plans. Keith, in fact, later did the same for the house. Basically, as far as a snooker club was concerned, I knew what I wanted. But you can never rush these things and the planning stage did turn out to be quite a long drawn-out affair. I had a firm of interior designers in to do some sketches and I must say it all looked very glamorous. But the budget was going through the roof. I did not mind losing money on the project, but there is a limit as to how far you can afford to go. So I dispensed with that idea. But in my mind a picture of the club was now forming. It was a very exciting time for me.

But then the whole project began to get me down. I had gone through that initial stage of enthusiasm and having had nearly three months of working twelve or fourteen hours a day non-stop, I was starting to feel dead inside. Unfortunately it rubbed off on Annette, because I would come home and, before I knew it, we were arguing about one thing or another. I was beginning to regret ever having taken on the task all by myself. It was never-ending. As soon as one person walked out of my office, someone else was waiting to walk in. And this went on everyday.

In the meantime there was a lot of doubt in my mind about the work I was giving out, because I knew so little about the business. For a start, I had no idea whether I was being charged a fair price or not, although it is surprising how quickly you learn and, on the positive side, by the end I felt I was an expert. First of all I started by giving out work on the basis of friends' recommendations. But then the word must have got out and a lot of people tried to take me for a ride. There was, of course, plenty of talk in the cafe among the workers there. 'Terry Griffiths is opening a club and needs some work done. He's got a few bob. Let's get in there.' One person in particular had a go, although fortunately I sussed him out straight away.

I was getting quotes for a new roof – and big job it was, too. So I was talking to this chap one day about it and he said he would do the job. I bumped into him a couple of days later and reminded him about it; I told him I needed a quote off him. 'Well, Terry, to do the job properly will be about £10,000.' At the time I thought it was a bit odd that he had not given me a written quotation like everyone used to, particularly for a job that size and with that sort of money involved. To be honest, the thing stank to me. I did not say anything then, but I got a few other quotes and finally had the roof done for £2,500! Obviously this guy had taken a look at me, thought about the job and just put any price on it, presumably thinking I might be stupid enough to accept it. It made me pretty mad to think someone could try to take advantage of me like that. I could understand people trying to get something out of it, since I was a beginner at all this. But I thought in this case they had gone too far.

He deserved to be taught a lesson and I decided I would get my own back when the time was right. I knew I would see him sooner or later over in the cafe, because he used the place quite a lot. Others wanted me to go and tell him straight away, but I wanted to catch him in my own time.

We went over to the cafe one morning and it was absolutely heaving. And who should be sitting there with some his workers? There were other roofers there, as well as plasterers and other builders – just the right crowd. So I went up to him – and I could see he knew what I was going to say. 'I had that roof done. £2,500 it cost me. £10,000 it was you quoted me, wasn't it?' There was silence. You should have seen his face. If you had hit him with a sledge-hammer, it would not have made more impact. The lads working for him looked so embarrassed and everyone else in the cafe heard what I had said. It had the desired effect.

If something needs to be said, I will just go up and tell the person to their face. I never used to be like that, but now I find it is the best way – to get it over and done with. I did not like what the fellow had done, but looking at it realistically I cannot blame him for trying. There were a lot of prices being paid in that club that were over the top. Eventually you start sussing them out. But that is life. If someone can get away with charging me £1000 for doing a £500 job, then the best of luck to him. If I agree to that price, that is my fault. I should know better. But because I have always had such a trusting nature, I expected people to give me the right prices, which did not actually happen. But this was all very good experience and helped make me a much harder person – particularly when it comes to business.

None of this, of course, helped improve my own mental state. The whole situation was getting on top of me and one day Annette and I had one hell of a row, which had obviously been brewing up. I told her that I could not handle it anymore without her moral support, at least. She did not have to be there but I needed her backing or else I could not do it. That helped clear the air. She could see I was getting into a bad state mentally. I was going home at night and not sleeping and then back to work the next morning with more jobs to do. And by now my head had virtually gone. I was coming to a stage when a breakdown was imminent, there was no doubt about it. I was feeling very similar to that time back in 1980 when I had that incident with Dennis Taylor at Cross Hands.

The problem now facing me was that I had to open the club before I started back on the circuit – the same situation that I had later with

141

the new house. Everyone wants to open a new business as quickly as possible, but in my case the reasons were slightly different. I had to open it before I went back on the road. If not, then I knew I could not have played. And that pressure was now starting to build, on top of everything else. One minute it looked as though you had plenty of time and then all of a sudden it had gone. Time was getting very tight and I felt myself being forced into a corner.

Throughout all this, we were pushing on with the construction of the club, but again everything seemed to take so long and nothing really got finished. Walls were going up, but they were not decorated. Nothing seemed to be knitting together. There were the usual delays on materials you get with any job. I found myself in a situation where I had to get a job finished but the parts were going to take ten days and there was two weeks' work involved. It was starting to get too much for me to handle and if it was not for those helping me out, I do not think I would have coped. Chris, John and Noel, especially, were a tremendous inspiration to me. They worked so hard and were full of encouragement. And I thought: If they can do that . . . And they would not take any money; they were doing it out of friendship.

Now the Far East Tour was coming up again. June and July had come and gone and time was running out. The place was finally taking shape, but we were faced with different headaches – like getting the carpet down and putting in the air-conditioning. And when you are trying to put the final touches to any project, everything suddenly becomes a major problem. But I was still determined to get the club open before the end of September – and we had set the 20th as the day, although nobody believed we could do it. I was adamant. I was going to open then. I did not care what happened. Even if people worked through the night, I was getting that club open. And that is what we had to do. We had everybody working flat out and, in fairness to them, they all made a fantastic effort.

Then the snooker season got underway and I was due to go to Scotland to play in the Laings. I was not concerned about the opening clashing with this since I did not expect to last long in the tournament. I really had not played any snooker during the summer, except on tour, because I had been in the club all the time and mentally I could not have been less prepared. I drew Neal Foulds in the first round and that proved quite an amusing sequence of events. I had booked the plane home the following day so that I could get back to the club because I knew I could not win. As things turned out, Neal had one of those days when he could not do a lot and I won 5–4. In the next round I had to play Jimmy White, so again I booked the plane home the following day since there was no way I was going to beat Jimmy. He was playing quite well, having won 5–0 in the previous round, and I could not pot a ball in practice, let alone play.

Incredibly I beat Jimmy. It was one of those things; everything was going in. I went for everything and got them all. I was convinced it was meant to happen. There was no way I could beat Jimmy that night, even if he had given me 40 start. But I did. Every time I hit the ball I thought: Good God, that went in. Jimmy admitted afterwards he could not do a lot; I just potted everything. I played very quickly that night and we finished the match in about 80 minutes which must be a world record for me.

So that meant another cancelled flight and this time a final against Joe Johnson. But more to the point, I was now going to miss the opening of the club, which was the day of the final. Although it was nice to have got there, in a way it was a terrible blow for me. We were only opening the doors – there was no official function – but I wanted to be there. I had not seen the last few things going together and could not picture the place finished. I had not seen the carpet on the floor.

Anyway, I played Joe and now it did not make any difference, I had missed the opening, so I had everything to play for. The irony of this was that I lost 9–7. So now I had not only missed the opening but also the trophy.

Now all I wanted to do was to get back to the club as quickly as possible. But I could not get a flight out. We had finished on the Sunday night and the Monday flight was full. So I booked a sleeper down to Birmingham where I had left my car. As soon as the match was over – about 10.30 in the evening – I dashed off to the station and jumped on the train. It was the first time I had ever taken a sleeper in my life. I arrived in Birmingham, took a taxi from New Street to the airport, got in the car and drove back to Llanelli. I arrived about four in the morning – just to look at the club. I could not wait to see what it was like finished. And when I did, in a way I wish I had not, because when I went in I had this horrible feeling of emptiness – seeing everything done after all those months.

The family had done a tremendous job in the weeks leading up to the opening of the club. By this time Annette had got heavily

143

involved and she and my father were there everyday helping out. And there I was, standing in the club they had finished, although I really had thought they would never do it. You get to the stage where you have done so much and everything had revolved round me – all the paperwork, the organisation, the ordering of materials, arranging the labour – and you get the feeling that nobody else can cope. As far as I was concerned there was no way they could manage without me and I had been on the phone from Scotland all the time trying to sort things out. But they had done it without me. As grateful as I was, it took me a few weeks to shake off that empty feeling. After all the work and mental stress of the summer, I suppose the reaction was understandable.

In the meantime, of course, I had to play professional snooker and it certainly was not going very well. Annette had said to me one day, 'What do you expect after what you've been through this summer?' And, of course, she was right. It would be wrong to put too much emphasis on the amount of work I did, but it was just I had never done anything like it before. From being a snooker player with a pretty easy life I had put myself under a different kind of stress and it was a massive mental upheaval in my life. Out of it all, apart from being a tremendous experience having to handle a project like this, I really appreciated more than anything the comradeship of the workers and the people I had got involved with; that was very important to me. It was certainly something I felt I had lost out of my life at the time, through being on the road playing snooker or at home spending time with the family. Because there is no comradeship on the professional circuit. You have friends, perhaps, but there is no comradeship. And that is something I really feel I had missed out on in life – for the last ten years anyway. That is really why I turned to local snooker again. It was able to give me back some of that – having a team of my own and supporting the players. It was to give me a sense of belonging that I had not had since I turned professional, and it was only then that I realised how much I had missed that side of life.

16 The Opening Night

NATURALLY I WANTED one of the Matchroom players to open the new club officially. In fact it was Jimmy White who approached me months before, when I was still pulling the place apart. 'When is your club opening, Tel? I'll come down and do it for you.' He was the first one to offer, although I think all the boys would have done so. It was a nice gesture. One or two people did, when they heard this, say to me, 'I think Steve Davis would like to open it more than anyone else.' I knew that, but Jimmy had offered first, which I was very chuffed about, and I saw no reason to put him off. Of course I would have been delighted for Steve to do the honours, too. But I am sure Steve understood and certainly would say nothing once he heard.

But over the months before the opening, I did begin to regret not having said something to Steve. I do not think it would have made any difference who was opening it. But deep down I knew Steve wanted to do it. Being the way he is, however, he waited for me to ask him. But it was too late for that, since Jimmy had already volunteered. Steve did keep on asking me when the opening was, which I felt embarrassed about.

So Jimmy was booked for the official opening, which we had decided to have in December, once the matchroom itself was finished and all the seating was in place. There was a tremendous buzz around Llanelli when the news got round that Jimmy was coming down, but this in itself created problems. During my career I have done so many club openings for different people and so I was naturally looking at it from a snooker player's rather than a business point of view. I suppose I should have invited hundreds of people to the opening, with Jimmy and I playing a few frames in the main arena and everyone milling about with a glass in their hand. But being a snooker player, I did not want that type of event for Jimmy. Because club openings can be one of the hardest jobs for a professional player, when you are expected to turn it on under appalling conditions, I wanted to arrange a match in the matchroom with just a 100 spectators – the capacity for sitting down. Otherwise everyone wanders about and chats away and there is little interest in the snooker. On reflection, this was probably a bad decision, but I took it for what I believed were the right reasons.

A few days before the big event, I went into the matchroom, which had just been finished, and sat down in one of the seats. I was on my own. I looked around the room, just trying to take it all in. It was very plush in there, a beautiful room with a pleasantly soft atmosphere – exactly what I wanted for a matchroom. Of all the places I had played in this for me was ideal. I started imagining what was there before – the stage of the Glen Ballroom where I had spent so many hours in my youth. People like Tom Jones and other stars of that period had performed on that very same spot. It was very nostalgic.

All of a sudden there was this realisation. I could not believe it was actually mine; it all seemed so unreal. Now it was finished, it really hit home to me. It was in a way as though my whole life was passing before me. I was by myself looking round the room and, at that moment, I felt I could stay there for ever. It was so soft and still – a perfect room for a game of snooker. But even if you had taken the table out, you would still not want to leave; there was so much peacefulness. Outside in the main club area there were ten tables all being played and opening the door and going out was like walking into another life. It was a very strange experience and I found tears coming to my eyes. I could not stop myself. I was glad nobody came in then.

One of the main reasons I had decided to have a club and create this matchroom as I did was prompted by an experience I had had the previous year, when Wayne played in the final of the town championship. I had gone to watch him in the Liberal Club, which was not ideal for an important match of this sort. It was a large room with a bar and two tables and, although I used to play there a lot as a youngster, I had not been there for a number of years.

I came out of there that night thinking: I wish the lads had a better place to play in. It was nothing against the club; after all, I was brought up in those places. But it was very restrictive and the facilities were non-existent. A bus load of supporters from Burry Port were there to cheer on Wayne's opponent John Edwards. It created a good atmosphere, but the playing conditions suffered badly. It was damp and full of smoke and the doors had to be opened between frames to help clear the air. Nobody could get served at the bar, either. But, more than anything else, the players had nowhere to sit down between shots. As a snooker player, I felt for both men, especially Wayne.

There were one or two incidents during the match when Wayne got in line with the shot and John complained to the referee that he was in his way. Wayne was very embarrassed and kept wiping his cue, which was getting very sticky because it was so humid. He had nowhere to go. There were no seats for the players and very little room to stand. Being a player, I know how uncomfortable that can be. And there was my son, only sixteen, and he was playing a chap I used to compete against in my amateur days. It was Wayne's first final and he was under a lot of pressure. John had won the title before and knew what it was all about. If Wayne did win, he would become the youngest ever to do so, beating my record by a month! John had a good following of supporters that night. Some of the crowd were behind Wayne, because he was so young. But there was a section that did not want him to win because he was my son.

So, when John complained to the referee about Wayne, I thought: This is it. Will Wayne collapse now or is he going to play better? I knew what he was going through; I had experienced the same myself. I could see his face going red. Either he was cracking up or getting the hump. Fortunately it was the latter and Wayne went on to win the match. I think that gave me more satisfaction – seeing Wayne win – than I probably got out of any of my own victories. Although it was only a local tournament, it was a very special occasion and gave me immense pride.

When we got home, Wayne slumped into a chair and did not say a word – just as I always did. Interestingly, I think that brought it home to Annette how I used to feel after winning an important tournament. She always used to comment that I never looked particularly happy. But seeing Wayne reacting in the same way, she appreciated what it takes out of you. All you really want to do is sit down with a cup of tea and say nothing. While there is the obvious pleasure of winning, unless you have competed at that level, it is hard to realise what it does take out of you. Mind you, I was just as bad that night. I was absolutely buzzing with Wayne's success, while he just sat quietly in the chair.

But that experience in the Liberal Club really convinced me to have a club with a proper matchroom where we could stage the finals of local competitions. It was not just so I could have my own setting and use it just for my own players, but also as a place for the local league, which had really set me up in my profession. Because that was where I learnt my trade. And that is why, as much as anything, I was sitting in that room with all the emotions and feelings that had, in a way, been realised.

The day of the official opening came and I was in a terrible state. Mainly I was worried for Jimmy's sake. I wanted everything to be right for him, because I knew there would be a lot of pressure on him, which I knew he was not keen on. To control the numbers, I had decided to keep the evening just for adults. But I knew the members would want their children to meet Jimmy. So I had this marvellous idea to invite a few kids in during the afternoon so they could see him and have their photograph taken with him. I do not know why, but I thought there would probably just be a handful who turned up and we would have them in and out in half-an-hour. In fact, fifty turned up and it was a shambles. Everyone was there – parents, aunts and uncles, grandparents, long-lost relatives . . . Now we were stuck and I did not know what to do. I did not want Jimmy to have to go through all this and realised I should never have asked him to do this in the first place. But Jimmy was as good as gold and handled the situation superbly, considering he is not too keen on this sort of thing because basically he is quite a shy person.

We finally finished the session and I whisked him back to his hotel to get some rest and prepare for the evening. In the meantime I was rushing round making sure everything was ready for the big occasion. The MC for the night rang me up to say his father had been taken ill and he would not be able to make it. I tried to get a last-minute substitute, but with no success, and finally decided to do the job myself.

One of my main concerns when I was arranging the opening was who to invite. There were obviously hundreds of people who wanted to come – and most of them were thoroughly entitled to a seat because of all the help they had given getting the place ready. But there was only room for a 100. I invited the mayor and other officials, as I felt I must, and managed to fit in quite a few who obviously deserved to be there. But sadly some had to be disappointed. Having got all that finally sorted out, Jimmy told me when he arrived that some mates of his were coming down from London for the evening. Now Jimmy has always got mates cropping up everywhere and naturally I wanted to make sure they were properly looked after, although heaven knows where they were going to sit. I asked him who they were. 'Oh, you know them,' he said. 'You've met them before. Boys from London.' I did not think any more about it.

Somehow we managed to get everyone seated and the evening got under way. I stood up and did the MC bit, offering a few words of thanks and introducing Jimmy. Then we got down to the snooker. It was a marvellous feeling – the first match in the matchroom and with a packed house. I hardly thought about the game. I was just soaking in the atmosphere.

We came to the interval and went out into the main club area for a short break. Then there was a buzz of excitement coming from the main stairs. I went over to see what was happening and got the shock of my life. Coming up the stairs were Barry, Robbo – and Steve. I was speechless. So these were Jimmy's mates from London!

Now I did not know what to do. There was Steve with his cue and I was saying, 'How did you get here?' Barry stood there laughing his head off. We went into the matchroom and immediately two of my friends offered their seats in the front row, which was great of them. Obviously I wanted Steve to play, but Jimmy had not managed any decent breaks in the first half and I wanted him to carry on and give the audience something to cheer about. He was trying so hard to make the night a success for me. Anyway, I said to Steve, 'What do you want to do?' Barry chipped in, 'Don't worry. He'll just play a frame with Jimmy at the end and do a few trick shots.'

So there we were. It was the big night and suddenly I had the two best players in the world in my small club in Llanelli. The same two players who, two weeks before, fought out one of the best-ever finals in the Tennants UK in Preston, which included five century breaks. It was one of the nicest things that has ever happened to me. What I

149

did not know was that all this had been planned months before. As soon as Steve found out I was having a club, he had said he would come down for the opening anyway. The fact that Jimmy had asked me made no difference to him. What made it even more special was that Steve had been ill with the flu and had got out of his sick bed to be here. As I stood there introducing the two of them, I was getting very emotional. I desperately wanted to say the right thing, but I could not find the words. Even now, thinking about it brings a lump to my throat.

Anyway, I got the second half going with a few words. I had to keep it as short as possible because I knew I was going to crack up. 'I suppose you have noticed the audience has changed slightly for the second half. I'm going to keep the introduction very short and just say, two of my best friends . . .' This was just what I felt about it and I could feel myself going. Do not ask me how, but I got through it and then went into the office where I cried my eyes out.

So that evening was a very emotional occasion all round. It was the fulfilment of all my dreams and plans. I had often thought how nice it would be to have a club in my home town, without ever thinking it was going to happen. But here it was and that realisation was incredibly difficult to take in. In a way, Barry summed it all up – as he normally does in such a situation, with a few well-chosen words when, after the club opening, I showed him the plans for the new house. 'Well, Griff, you haven't done badly for a postman, have you?' And it was right. He was saying what he really felt about it all. And I felt the same way, too, I was not a postman; I was a professional snooker player. But when I think back to those times – the Llanelli League and all that – and what I have got now, it is all there in my club.

A lot of people have said to me since, 'It's nice that you have put your money back into the town.' But that is not strictly true; I would be lying if I said that. I put it back into the town because I love the town. But it is not for the town; it is for me. Put money back into snooker in the town, yes . . . I'd like to say that, because snooker in the town is important to me. It is where I grew up, where I spent the first sixteen years of my snooker career and where I learnt my trade, playing one frame every Wednesday night. I gained a tremendous amount from all that – from the other players, by competing against them, week in, week out.

But I always thought that snooker in Llanelli was not going forward enough, mainly because they were still playing the big matches in clubs where the facilities were not quite up to the mark. And I suppose to most people in Llanelli, they did not see anything wrong with that. But I had been round the country and seen other matchrooms and venues where they played local finals and I had decided I wanted a place like that in Llanelli. I felt there was a gap there that needed filling.

Going back, I think it was watching that final with Wayne and experiencing the conditions they were playing in – not just Wayne but John as well. I was brought up like that, playing finals in such situations, and of course at the time I did not see anything wrong with it – I knew no better in those days. But then I had seen the other side of the snooker world and felt things should now be better for the local lads.

17 A Family Investment

NATURALLY I FELT a great sense of pride in my new club. It had turned out a lot better than I thought it would, which is unusual because often things do not come out as well as you hoped. But then I found myself getting into a position where I was embarrassed about it. People would come in – old school friends, playing mates, old amateur players, people I had had a lot of respect for in the earlier days – and they were lashing me with praise. And all of a sudden I did not want to be there. It was a bit overwhelming and it embarrassed me. Being in my own town, in my own club, I had been feeling more settled in my mind – away from the professional scene. But with these people saying how beautiful the club was and how well I had done brought the professional side back to me.

For the first few weeks in the club people kept coming in and I was offering to show them round. I wanted everyone to see the place. But I quickly stopped doing that because I felt so uncomfortable about it. Curiously it was beginning to pull me away from my roots again – one of the very reasons for having the club in the first place. It was putting me on a different plane to see the rest there and I did not want that to happen. Just because it was my club, that should not matter. I wanted to be part of it, which I have done. But when visitors came in, especially players whom I used to compete against and lose to, I found it hard to accept that they were now looking at me in a totally different way.

I do not think there is any real resentment over the club, anymore so than my success generally. But human nature being what it is, a lot of people were jealous of my success as a professional and would probably extend this to the club. But I would like to think that the majority of those who know me are proud of what I have done in snooker. That is life, of course, and you have got to accept it for what it is. Those things do not bother me in the slightest anymore. They used to in the earlier days, but now I take them with a pinch of salt. I have found from the experiences I have had as a professional that if people want to come up and criticise me, I will happily talk to them about it and accept it for what it is. But if they cannot tell me what they think to my face, then I have not got the time of day for them.

There is no doubt it used to worry me when I was younger, but over the years I have hardened up a lot. You get criticism and rightly so when you are in the limelight. If you play badly, you deserve to be criticised. But there have been times when people have knocked me unfairly. I have not really said much about it, but sometimes it hurts.

Jealousy may well have crept in over the fact that the club has been very successful on the playing side. The teams we have got have done very well so far, which gives me a lot of satisfaction. I have also managed to get better prize money for local snooker, which has never been done before. The Buckley Brewery helped sponsor the club and has supported me ever since. Last year they put up £2000 in prize money – £1000 first prize. They had never even seen prize money before in Llanelli. So you can imagine with my team winning there was bound to be some resentment. But what can you do? Don't put up prize money? Don't build a club?

Because of my interest in local snooker and my ambition to run not only a successful but happy club, there are bound to be times when I probably overdo things. For example, I have been told more than once that I spoil the youngsters there. Possibly that is true, although generally that is not something that would worry me. However there was one occasion recently when I had no choice but to put my foot down.

It all revolved around the van we had, which we used to use to take Darren's scrambling bike to meetings. Instead of selling it when the bike went, I decided it would be quite useful around the club and in fact offered it to the players on match nights to ferry people about. On this particular night the team had a match, but the van had already gone. What had happened was I had entered a father and son team in a doubles tournament – and paid for it – and

153

they had decided they were going to use the van. When I rang them and asked for it back, they said, 'Well, we won't bother to play, then.' I could not believe it. Anyway, I decided that would not happen again. I got rid of the van.

I do sometimes wonder whether all the effort the family puts in to the club in terms of organising the leagues and competitions is really appreciated. We did go through a spell where some of the players did not bother to practise and were not putting much effort into matches. But those are phases every club suffers from and on the whole they are a pretty good bunch of lads.

In terms of the club itself, I have done a lot of things inside that reflect the fact that I am a player. If I had approached it simply from a business point of view, it would certainly have turned out differently. For example, the bar area would have been separate. But I did not want that. I had been brought up in the old style snooker club, with the bar alongside the tables. And all the good players used those tables because everyone there would watch them.

Decisions like that I must admit I took for selfish reasons, because they were things I wanted myself. After all, it was my club – rather our club, since the family has been very much involved in it too. But that is not to say I regret any of it. When I go round and visit other clubs, where the decor is nothing very special and often the tables are pretty rough, they are still doing tremendous business. Of course their outlay has been minimal and they have spent very little money on the place. In contrast I went for a very plush club, which perhaps was not the best idea.

In many ways I feel the club is probably too posh for this area. I find a lot of people who come in feel it is not the sort of place they want to play snooker in; because snooker is still basically a working man's game and always will be. You can forget all the plush professional arenas, the big money and the glamour of television. It is a working man's game and working class people often do not like going into a place where they have got to use the ashtrays. They cannot feel comfortable in posh surroundings. That is no disrespect to them. I grew up in that type of snooker hall. But, unlike me, people in our part of the world are not generally very receptive to the idea of change.

On the other hand, Annette, myself and the boys could not have been comfortable in an old-style snooker club. I have to be truthful with myself and admit that circumstances have changed my attitude to certain things in life. We have now got used to a higher standard of living and I would not expect my family to accept anything less. And it was very important to me that the family did get involved in the club. That was one of the main reasons I started it. Annette particularly needed to have an involvement in something else. She comes away with me quite regularly now, but there are still a lot of nights when she would otherwise be at home on her own and I knew she had always wanted to have her own business. She had spoken about it a lot, perhaps opening a hairdresser's or a clothes shop. But she did not want a full-time job. So a further reason for taking on a club was to provide Annette with another interest. It was also partly for the children to have something later on in life.

I thought it was important to get Annette involved as heavily as possible while the club was getting established. And she has done that. During the first year she spent a tremendous amount of time there, to the extent that it started to get her down; it was proving too much. Now we have reached the happy stage where she can go in for a few hours when she wants. Another advantage is that she has made friends with a lot of members there, which you necessarily do in a club. So if she feels a little bored sitting at home she can come up to the club for a few hours and work at the bar or chat to the members.

The other great satisfaction is that Wayne now more or less runs the place for us. He had done pretty well at school and had just passed his 'O' levels the summer we opened. Because he has always been very keen on snooker and plays well, too, I personally was only too pleased for him to come into the club. But the decision was a hard one to make. Should he stay on at school, do his 'A' levels and perhaps go on to university or further education? That summer he had talked about training to be an airline pilot and we had got a lot of information through from Steve Davis's girlfriend Judy, who works for British Airways. But he started wavering when he discovered that he had to have some 'A' levels, which he thought might prove too difficult to get. If he had decided that was what he wanted, we would not have stood in his way. Neither Annette nor I believe in telling the children what to do; it is up to them.

But now Wayne could see the club taking shape, added to which all the friends in the team he played for wanted to come and join our club. So Annette and I had to decide whether Wayne's heart was ruling his head. Would it be better for him to stay on and finish his education? What really swayed it for me was that Wayne used to spend a lot of time in his bedroom swotting for exams. He did very well, but I thought about what might happen if he spent another two years shut away studying and did not get his 'A' levels. He would have lost two years of his life, in my opinion. Of course, the club was going to him anyway, eventually. But one day we had a long chat about it and finally he said he would rather come in to the club. Annette was not totally keen on the idea. That probably stemmed from the fact that she did not have that much of an education. For her, school was always a matter of serving time, something to get through. She has regretted that she did not manage to get any qualifications and obviously wanted Wayne to get a better start in life.

Wayne left school in July and came straight into the club, which of course was being pulled down and put up again at that time. That is not quite how he would have arranged it, since he wanted his summer holidays first. He was quite put out when I cancelled them. But he did get stuck in and was a great help, considering the fact that he was still only sixteen.

For the first nine months in the club I was looking after all the business side such as the ordering of stock, the paperwork and the accounts, which was a lot of work. I was also organising the tournaments and other snooker activities within the club, which took up the rest of the time I had. Again there was no let-up. I was there all hours of the day, sometimes only finishing at midnight and then returning early the next morning. This was, of course, when I was at home. The problem came when I was away playing snooker. After a while I decided it was time to give Wayne more responsibility, which he took to very well.

Wayne was definitely getting bored just serving behind the bar. It was not what he wanted to do. So I took the plunge and showed him how to do the paperwork, the banking and the general book-keeping – and he took to it just like that. Certainly it made a great difference to his attitude and now he appreciates the club a lot more. He sees what the takings are – up and down – and knows everything that is going on within the club. It has given him a real interest and a sense of responsibility, which lads of that age need, I am sure.

I shall never forget the first week I showed him what to do with the accounts. He has got a good head for figures and took to the books very quickly. But what struck me most was that I had never seen the office looking tidier. This was very satisfying and proved how much he cared for the job and wanted to keep it organised. He knew there was an opportunity for him at the club and he grasped it.

After all that had gone in getting the club together, you would have thought I had had enough for a while. But last year I had the chance of buying another club in Llanelli. The thinking behind that was that it would be something for Darren once he had left school.

There has obviously been some friction between the two boys, which you will always get in this situation. Being the older son, Wayne always had first choice and the first chance at everything. He had the first car, the first job . . . and that is how life is. I suffered the same as Darren, because I was the younger brother, too.

Running two clubs would pose problems, but I would like to think it could have worked. I would not have made the second one anything like the Matchroom or of the same standard. It would have been much more low key. Any thoughts and plans for it were, alas, premature, since the deal fell through. Not that I see it as a major set-back, since Darren knows he can always come and work in the Matchroom when he leaves school, if that is what he wants.

Both Annette and I were very conscious of the fact that while we were working on the club we were neglecting Darren a lot. Wayne got involved because he was that much older and obviously interested in the snooker aspect. But Darren was being left in the house and I was hardly ever seeing him. I was off to the club early in the morning as Darren went to school and often he would be in bed by the time I got back in the evening. Although we did bring him into the club during the holidays to help out, he was really still too young to get fully involved. It was even worse when the club opened, because Annette started coming in every night as well. I do not think Darren minded too much about the situation because he is the sort of lad who is quite happy with his own company. But it did worry us for a while.

Wayne had always been keen on sport and played a great deal of soccer as well as snooker, which I enjoyed going to watch. I also went to see Darren play soccer and rugby at school when I could, but over the last few years he has not bothered so much with team

157

sports. He did take up scrambling, which neither Annette nor I were particularly keen on because it was quite dangerous. We were always frightened he would have a bad accident. Even when my free time was very limited, I used to go with him as much as I could. I might only be home for a day between engagements, but I would always make the effort, because I was conscious I had not spent enough time with either of my sons. That was not entirely my fault, of course, since snooker had kept me away so much. Sometimes Darren would come in the car with me when I went out locally, but he hardly said a word. He just enjoyed sitting there. Wayne takes after me and is much more sport orientated, so we naturally find a lot more to talk about.

When I had my motorbikes, Darren and I would sometimes go out for a ride together. To begin with he was always falling off and spent more time on his backside than on the bike. And everytime he fell off I would have a heart attack. He broke his collar bone one day practising in the woods; he came off the bike and hit a tree. He has also fractured his wrist. But it never worried him. He really enjoyed the scrambling and getting up on the line for a race was something special to him. So Annette and I persevered with it, despite the fact that it was not only dangerous but very expensive. Apart from the bike and all the equipment you needed, we had to have a van to take everything around in. And, of course, there were constant repairs on the bike itself.

What with all the time being spent in the club, we were not able to go to meetings so often and, although a friend's parent offered to take him, we did not think it was fair to land them with the responsibility, should anything happen to Darren. So we had to tell him he could not race as much, which we hated doing. His only comment was, 'That's all right, as long as I can keep the bike to practise on and just go now and again.' Good old Darren; he was so easy going. This made it easier for us from a practical point of view, but harder to accept in other ways. We felt we were taking advantage of his willingness to accept everything so readily.

One weekend when I was home, I offered to take him racing because I knew how much he wanted to go, particularly since all his mates were taking part that day. Annette wanted him to pack it in there and then, but I wanted him to make that decision for himself. He had not practised very much, so I did not expect him to do very well. After a few races I think he realised that, without going regularly, there was not much point in doing it because he was not going to win. And I could see he was not enjoying it as much as he used to. When we later suggested selling the bike, he agreed. In return, we bought him a racing cycle, because he was now getting interested in cycling. We found a buyer for the other bike, who came round and took everything while Darren was at school. We thought it would be too upsetting if he was there when it all went. That was a strange feeling, rather like getting rid of the family pet. But we had agreed it was better that way.

Darren then joined Bynea Cycling Club and went bike racing, which he quite enjoyed. And by this time he was also playing squash. But even cycling can be hazardous, as we were soon to find out. Just recently he went off to the Gower Peninsula, which is about 30 miles away, to watch some racing. He had been gone a few hours when the phone rang, 'Can you come and pick me up? I'm in hospital.' Annette had answered the phone and went into a panic about what had happened. All Darren said was that he had had an accident and would be waiting in the out patients department for us. Then he put the phone down. In the meantime Annette and I were having a heart attack worrying about him.

When we got there, he was sitting on his own with blood all over him. Apparently he had come round a bend too fast, could not stop and had hit a car. He had scrapes all over his legs and stitches in his hands. But despite all that, he was his normal cheerful self and shrugged the whole incident off, despite the fact that he was in agony. When we got him home he went to bed, but he was up the next morning ready to go to school. That is Darren.

18 A Dream Come True

ONE OF MY MOST satisfying achievements has been the building of our new home, which I look on as the culmination of a life's work and effort for both Annette and myself. It certainly seems a lifetime away when we borrowed some money off my father to buy our first home – a terraced property in Island Place in the middle of Llanelli. It has since been knocked down and is now a car park. That cost us £1500. From there we moved to a modern semi-detached in Swiss Valley, which was really up-market. We paid £9,500 for one of the new dormer-style bungalows for young married couples. It was a great thrill for both of us moving there – something special.

Winning the World Championship in 1979 changed many things in our life and significantly enabled us to buy a 'dream home' in Pembrey, a superb detached house which even had a snooker room, That cost £37,500, which seemed a fortune to us. We lived there from January 1980 and were very happy in it. The house was a good size, with as I have said its own snooker room and plenty of garden for the boys. That was the main thing for me, because I had never had a garden as a child and I always wanted Wayne and Darren to have one. We spent many hours on the big lawn at the back playing soccer and cricket.

Although we loved that house and spent several happy years in it, Annette and I had both been thinking about building a larger place to our own design and hopefully where we could enjoy more of the spectacular views you get around that part of Wales. Because we had settled down in Pembrey, we therefore agreed to try to find a piece of land in the immediate area. The location is magnificent, with the golf course and forest, and you can look out across these to the Gower Peninsula and the sea.

So we had a good hunt round and must have seen loads of different plots of land. Either they were not suitable or were not available or we could not get planning permission on them. I did buy a few pieces here and there in desperation, just in case the authorities relented. But none of them were really ideal.

Then eventually we found the piece of land on which we have now built. It was part of two fields covering about fifteen acres above Pembrey, up on the hill almost behind our old house. It was an ideal spot, just off the road, with a magnificent view across the forest out towards the Gower. One of the major local developers had tried to build a housing estate there, but had been turned down by the local council. The first time we went to have a look at it, I remember walking through a gap in the hedge and all of a sudden the whole panorama opened up in front of us. It was a breath-taking experience. And I shall never forget the sounds that day; the only thing you could hear were the birds. As I stood there taking it all in, I thought: This spot is absolutely perfect.

When we first enquired about it, the development plans had already been submitted. But as soon as we heard they had been turned down, we approached the owner. He was quite happy to sell us an acre of the field, as long as we got planning permission and did not block any of his entrances. Naturally we were thrilled, but we still had to overcome a major hurdle – persuading the planners to give the go-ahead since the site was in a Green Belt area. To be fair, the town council was very helpful. I think it realised that I wanted to build a very substantial property which would help the environment rather than disturb it. The fact that I had stayed in the area and had not moved out after my success in the early years, I believe, also made the council more sympathetic.

Things got going in about May 1987. Annette and I must have spent literally hundreds of hours planning it all out, with the help of Keith Hughes again, since I had been very pleased with the way he had handled the club. Believe it or not, the inspiration for the house came from a London tube station! Perhaps I should explain.

Annette and I were coming out of the underground during one of our visits to London and happened to spot a poster for one of the main property developers. On it was this elegant Georgian-style executive home and we immediately fell in love with it. After that, I saw it a few times in different stations and each time I thought: That has got to be the basis of our new house. It is odd to think that one of the most depressing places in the world gave us the inspiration we needed.

Being of Georgian style, the house would fortunately blend in well with the environment round Pembrey. I am sure that if we had wanted a Tudor property, for example, we may well have had our application turned down because it would have been completely out of character for that area. One of the problems was that from the country park and the entrance to the beach, where we get thousands of visitors every year, the house is very much in view. So you could understand the council's point of view. Nobody wanted a house that would stick out like a sore thumb.

From May onwards, it was all a bit tortuous. Everything seemed so slow in developing and I think it was about October before any bricks went up. It was very frustrating. We would go up to have a look and nothing was happening. Of course there was always a perfectly good reason for the inactivity. The builder was being held up, deliveries were late . . . the same old stories. Then, towards the end of the year, it started to come together and we were given a moving-in date for January. Obviously, as time went on, we knew they were not going to make it – not by a long way.

You would have thought, after all the experiences of the club, that I would have left well alone this time. Not a bit of it! Apart from which, I was obviously now a lot more knowledgeable and wiser about these things. I negotiated a contract with Peter Davis, who is a director of a company called 'Up-date', to supply the kitchen and bedrooms in return for doing a television advertisement and some in the local press for three years. I sorted out the electrics with the lads who had done the club – and it was the same with the plumbers. So I was taking a lot of work off the main builders and gradually this got more and more as we neared completion. The builders were having some difficulties with their sub-contractors, since now they were on to the smaller jobs and there was little money coming through. In the end I told them I would carry on, so I was now doing the foreman's job on site as well.

During all this, there was an episode with the roofing company, who had asked me if I would like an aerial photo of the house. The scheme was that if I allowed it to be used for publicity purposes, I would get £150. Naturally I wanted to know exactly how the house was going to be used and was told it was for brochures and other advertising – and I was also expected to provide a few words of recommendation. When I queried the amount, I was told it was their normal budget for that sort of thing. 'If you want to take pictures of the house, then it's £500 and no words,' I said. I was paying them thousands of pounds for the work and all they were offering me in return were a few hundred so that they could use my name. What a cheek!

Anyway, having lost the summer of '87 with building the club, I was now losing the summer of '88 as well, this time with the house. And history was repeating itself. I was getting there at eight in the morning and staying till late at night. Having rushed round all day ordering materials, giving the lads their jobs and checking what was being done, I would then spend the evening cleaning up inside after they had gone home. Like the club, it all seemed never-ending. There was always something that needed my attention. But finally it all came together and by July we were in.

That was an enormous relief, I can tell you. But now my summer was almost over and yet again I had lost my holiday. I think with the club as well the year before, this really bothered me. The trouble was I should never have done the house and the club at the same time; they actually started together. In fairness, the house was already being thought about when the club came up – and I had to take that straight away otherwise somebody else might have stepped in. If that had happened, I could not have opened another club. Three in Llanelli would have been too many. But it was very unfortunate timing, having both places to worry about at the same time.

Again, the house turned out much better than we thought. In fact, it is more like a show house. We had an interior designer in to create the colour schemes, which help set it off so well. There is no doubt it is a lovely home. But, similar to the club, I felt for the first month or so I could not settle down to it. For a start, workers were still busy finishing off bits and pieces, which provided constant harrassment. Also, after all the months of putting the house together, I found it difficult to appreciate. It was my fault, I know. I got too involved in it all – and too early. Apart from the actual building, Annette and I had been looking for various things for the house for months beforehand – things like carpets, curtains and tiles.

As a result, I was worrying about the pending snooker season and trying to clear my mind for that, which of course did not happen. Curiously, however, I was for the first time actually looking forward to going away on the Far East Tour. I could not wait to get away – and I told Annette so. Considering how I normally feel about travelling abroad, this was ironic.

It was the old problem of getting too involved in everything. Being me, I had to see what everyone was doing all day – chasing this, chasing that – and on top of putting up with all the normal hiccups you get with a building and things going wrong. People had warned me that when you build your own house, there are always problems with the builders. I am sure they are always there, the only difference is that you never see them if you buy a house that has been completed.

Even now I find it hard to settle in the house, because it is so different to anything we have been used to. I think my father summed it all up perfectly when he first saw it. I sat him down in front of the television by the patio doors so he could see the magnificent view and poured him a cup of tea. All he could say was: 'This is like a bloody hotel.' My father will always say what he thinks and really that is what I felt about it too. Again my roots were eating at me. To be honest, the house probably is too posh. And thinking about it took me back to the days of my youth, when we used to go round houses just like this one knocking on doors on Guy Fawkes Night or when singing carols at Christmas. They were the big houses on the hill, where the rich people lived. And now here I was, one of them. It is sometimes very hard to accept that.

It would be wrong to make too much of all this, because deep down I really love the place. But we have become a major attraction. People keep driving up and looking at the house from the front gate. There are always cars full of faces staring and pointing. And when friends come inside, they tend to say, 'Good God, look at the size of this room . . .' I feel bad enough about it as it is, without others reminding me. Funnily enough, Annette loves the place. I had expected her to be more like the others, but she has really taken to the house and thinks it is tremendous – which of course it is. That is very important to me. If Annette had not settled, it would have been very difficult – what with me being away so much of the time.

I suppose my feelings for the house – and the club for that matter – stem from the fact that I find it very difficult to accept the position I now enjoy in life. Mentally I am fighting against it all the time. The early months of planning the house were tremendously exciting. But so much has gone into it and so much money spent. And again, I think a lot of the money side of it, not just the house but the club as well. It is all so unreal. They are things that even ten years ago I would not have dreamed about. There is no doubt as far as I am concerned that the way you have been brought up is the way you are.

Obviously it has been very different for the boys, since the environment they have been brought up in is such a contrast to the one Annette and I were used to. They have their own bedrooms, with television and telephone which we did not even have in our house when I was a boy. There is a bathroom with a jacuzzi, too. I must admit I love all these luxuries, but it is great that the kids can have them, too. Interestingly, they seem to accept it more readily, although that is understandable since they have experienced more of the good life and have probably got used to it. Most of their life has been spent while I have been a professional snooker player and they did not know much about the earlier times when we had to scratch for every penny.

It is sometimes hard for Annette and I to understand the way the boys think. Annette is always saying they do not appreciate what they have got, but I am sure they do in their own way. It is just that they have been brought up to a different way of life. We have tried to keep them on a level as best we can – educating them at local schools, for example. We bought a house in Pembrey that was near a council estate so that they could grow up with the type of children we wanted them to mix with. But, at the end of the day, they will always be Terry Griffiths' sons. And that in itself gives them more problems than they would otherwise have had. Children look at them and treat them differently, although now they are old enough to cope with this.

I often wonder now, with the house and the club and the family grown up, if I will keep on setting up challenges for myself. Annette has said to me that it is about time we called a halt. I suppose professional snooker is enough of a challenge in itself and the house and club are things I have brought upon myself to counteract that, since until recently snooker had completely dominated my life. I believe I had to take on these challenges, despite the fact that it has affected my performances on the table, because I felt I was getting in a rut. That is really what all this is about. I got to the stage where I had had success – and failure. Every season I would start again. Then it became a hard slog. Perhaps next year I will do something else. Who knows?

The club can still take up a lot of my time, if I allow it to, what with promoting competitions and coaching. It is simply a matter of how much I want to do there. At least I am not tied to it seven days a week any more and therefore the enjoyment of it should last a long time. There was a period when I did not want to go to the club, a similar feeling to that I had with the house. I had put so much into it and it had in return taken over so much of our family life that I did feel some resentment towards it. I think Annette felt a bit of that, too, because she had to work so many hours in the first year. But now she can go there occasionally, which is ideal.

Wayne is coping very well with the business and that has taken a lot off my shoulders. Although I go in to give him a hand when he needs it, normally I can relax, have a chat, watch the lads playing and have a game or two myself. I have been playing quite a lot up there recently, which I had not been doing for some time.

Looking back, I have probably done more in the last couple of years than in the rest of my life. It would be wrong to say I had not got any satisfaction out of it, because I have. Take the house. Everytime I drive up the road I look forward to seeing it and when I pull in the drive I still think the place is gorgeous. And it is the same with the club. When I go in and see all the lads playing – and possibly there is a big match on – it is very fulfilling. When Jimmy and Steve came for the opening night, all of a sudden I felt what all the other people there were feeling – Jimmy White and Steve Davis in the same room playing snooker was like a lifetime's dream come true. And the faces of everyone in the matchroom that night are something I shall never forget. Within that room, that night, it all came out as one – what had happened with the club and my snooker life. And with Barry there as well, it really brought it home to me. Barry never said a word that night; he just sat there. And Steve, too, just played his game and did some trick shots. I had asked Barry if he wanted to say anything, but he declined. Steve got up and admitted he felt a twinge of jealousy about the club, which I know he does. He would like a club, but he knows from what I have gone through that it requires a great deal of involvement. But that in itself I gain enormous satisfaction from.

19 The Price of Success

SUCCESS IN ANY walk of life is naturally relative. I shall always be grateful for my skill on the snooker table, for the money I have earned has allowed us as a family to have and do so much more.

When I was working as an insurance agent, up until I turned professional, I was earning between £3500 and £4000 a year. In contrast, after I won the World Championship in 1979, I was charging £200 a night, working five or six nights a week and was fully booked. That year I earned £75,000 which was then fabulous money for me.

Considering the complete change it all made to my life, it is strange that within a couple of years I had grown quite used to the money.

When I joined Barry Hearn in 1982, I doubled my earnings and was then making around £150,000 a year – and all that with about half the work I was doing before.

It is interesting to compare the difference ten years makes. The World Championship in 1979 was worth about £10,000. And I picked up £3000 for winning the Benson and Hedges the following year. Now you get £6750 just for turning up, which works out at about £130 a week for one game! By winning just one match you get £13,000. Currently I would expect to earn £200,000 – and charge £2000 a night. Today's top players are guaranteed around £100,000 without winning a single title. And if they do pick up a few titles, then there is the potential to earn £1/2 million.

People always talk about the glamour that comes with success and I cannot deny that even in snooker we get our fair share. Personally I try to avoid it, but it is very difficult to keep out of the spotlight all the time.

One aspect that inevitably comes with such success is women – and in this respect snooker is no different from any other popular sport. There are the girls who follow some of the players – Kirk Stevens and Tony Knowles, for example, and more recently Stephen Hendry. This is hardly surprising since the game does attract a large female audience. But that is not all about snooker; it seems women like the way players present themselves, too.

Fortunately the fans I attract seem to accept me for what I am – a family man. I am certainly not the playboy type. I do not go to pubs or clubs or go out in the evenings during tournaments. One of the nice things, however, is that I get lots of good luck cards and presents like teddy bears and rabbits when I play, which I really appreciate.

Annette used to get quite concerned about what I might be getting up to when I was away. But she has learnt to accept that I do not get involved. At the end of the day it is all down to trust.

When you are in the public eye so much, you do tend to create an image which becomes your trademark. In my case, it is my hair. I suppose I laid myself open to this by changing the style so many times. But the simple answer is that it is just part of me and my nature. I have had a lot of publicity through it over the years – and not all of it very pleasant – but it really does not bother me.

There was one incident that really got out of hand and was very upsetting at the time. It was to do with the hairdresser I use at home – a mate called Michael. Rumours first started when I was seen with him on several occasions in Llanelli. Quite simply, because I was home so little, and then often for just a few hours, Michael used to come round to the house to do my hair, and Annette's for that matter. More often than not, this was in the evening. I was very grateful to Mike because I just did not have the time to go into the salon during the day.

But eventually the rumours were spreading like wildfire and suddenly the story was in the national press. I then started to realise that a rumour turned to fact in most people's minds once it had been passed on by five or six people. Of course, it is still a rumour for all that.

To start with it was a bit of a joke. Then it all got rather serious. A feature writer from one of the cheap Sundays – Sue Bishop – did an interview with me at the Grosvenor Hotel during a WPBSA golf day at Sheffield. I remember asking Len Ganley to be with me, since I am always wary of feature writers. She mentioned all the local rumours and then wrote a typical denial story – 'Terry Griffiths is not gay'. It was an appalling piece in which she even quoted Annette out of context.

The next thing I knew the television cameras were outside. I refused to say anything. I had completely lost confidence in the press. I could stand it, but it was not fair on the family or Michael. Friends were busy giving me advice, but I made no comment at the time. Personally I did not care too much about my national image, but I did care what people were saying locally.

Eventually I decided to do an exclusive story with the local paper, the Llanelli Star, and had the whole front page one week. I was very hurt about it all. These were my people and it was my home. I basically said how narrow-minded Welsh people can be sometimes. They still think that if a woman goes into a pub alone she must be a prostitute and if a man has a perm he must be gay. God, in that case there must be thousands of prostitutes and gay men about in Llanelli.

In a way I feel sorry for people like Sue Bishop. She is a typical feature writer, always under pressure from her editor to get a story. Foremost in their minds is the famous maxim: make sure the facts don't get in the way of a good story. The problem is that if you live in a jungle long enough you will turn into an animal. She had concocted the whole story out of a rumour and really could not care less.

I did feel the effects of it for a while. Just after Dennis joined us, we were in Manchester for a photo session. In fact, it was the day after the golf dinner, I believe. The following day I was appearing in the Pontins Professional in front of the whole snooker world and that got to me a bit. I made a speech at the end, after I had won the tournament, and said, 'I hope I will make tomorrow's papers with something that's actually happened.' A big cheer went up, which made me feel a lot better.

I got a lot of sympathy – and letters – from people in Llanelli after that local article appeared. I had thought very carefully about what to say in the feature and fortunately it seemed to have paid off.

Going back to my hairstyle, it does reflect me in many ways. I like to be a perfectionist both in my play and my appearance, which includes my clothes and, of course, my hair. I have, I agree, gone

169

from one extreme to the other. In the early years I did not even have a suit to my name. Then, after joining Matchroom, I used to be a standing joke, since I never turned up for anything without a suit on. I have relaxed that now. I will turn up looking a lot more casual, but still smart, I hope.

Another obvious effect of being in the public eye is the problem of travelling around. Since 1979 I have tried to avoid using public transport for that reason. If you become a public figure and decide to travel in public, then you have to accept that people will come up to you all the time. If you find it particularly annoying or embarrassing, then you should not expose yourself.

If, for example, I do travel on a train and there are forty people in the carriage, those I would happily talk to never bother you. They are a lot more understanding. But unfortunately there are always those who won't leave you alone – the more loutish type who do not carry on the sort of conversation I would want and never know when to go away. Others might approach you, but at least they know when to leave.

I remember reading a quote from a television personality once, which really says it all. From what I recall, he said, 'You spend all your life working hard to be famous. And when you become famous, you spend the rest of your life working hard to escape from it.' That is so very true.

But fame does have its lighter and brighter sides, such as the odd invitations you get that can prove very enjoyable. Last year my local cricket club, Burry Port, asked me if I would play a few games for the second team. The first match was rained off and in the next game I scored 20 runs. A local press photographer was there and I had my picture in the Llanelli Star – for making 20! Ridiculous! People even talked about my playing for the first team. Wayne said to me afterwards. 'Aren't you embarrassed being in the paper when you only scored 20?' I had to admit I was a bit.

Maybe justice was done when I played for the Matchroom team against some local journalists in Romford. I bowled eight overs that day and took 5 for 21. I was shattered afterwards and, what made it worse, never got a mention in the local paper!

Talking of cricket, I have played a few celebrity games for the Lord's Taverners and I remember one against an Old England XI when John Jameson hit the ball very hard straight at me at mid-off.

Gosh, did that hurt! Later in the match Fred Truman slung a ball down at Steve Davis, who was also playing. The ball was in the keeper's hands before Steve had even lifted his bat. When Fred was asked to slow it down a bit, he replied, 'But I'm not even bowling medium pace these days. I don't know what's the matter with these boys.' Fortunately they put a spinner on the next over.

I have always enjoyed playing sport of all kinds and, belatedly, took up golf in 1984 at the Ashburnham Golf Club, which is just down the road from where we live in Pembrey. It is a links course, and a very difficult one, but really enjoyable to play. I had a series of lessons from Richard Playe, the professional there, who incidentally is now my next-door neighbour. For the first two or three summers I used to play all the time, which I think started to annoy Annette, since I would be away playing snooker all winter and then be out on the course playing golf most of the summer when I was home.

By 1986 I was playing off a 12 handicap, which I am sure I could have improved on, but I just could not play enough. And with my commitment to the club in 1987 and the new house in 1988, my handicap has slipped back to 18. I have certainly missed my golf and hope to have more time to play in the future.

I have had lots of invitations to play in Pro-Am tournaments and charity events, which I thoroughly enjoy, and I remember actually winning one tournament, a Cathay Pacific event in Richmond Park near London. The Australian golfer Graham Marsh was there, which was a great thrill for me. He actually came round the course with me.

The problem was that Cathay Pacific had organised the event for their customers and since the company also sponsored Matchroom with flight tickets for the Far East Tour it was not quite cricket for me to win. So I agreed to give up my prize for one of the customers.

My only other success was at a tournament at Wenvoe Castle near Cardiff. When I got home, I told Wayne that I had won a trophy. He went out to find it in the boot of the car and was quite disappointed when he saw this tiny runners-up cup. But it meant a lot to me.

I really enjoy playing golf and certainly regret not having taken up the game earlier. One interesting thing about playing is that because I am not and never will be that good at it, I can realise and appreciate the talent I have for snooker.

Another aspect of being a snooker star that I have also thoroughly enjoyed is appearing on television when I am off the table. Over the years of being a professional, I have done so many things on television other than playing that it turns you into a personality rather than a snooker player, which to begin with I found quite strange.

Obviously the big one was This Is Your Life. Then I went on to do the BBC Sports Review of the Year, which of course Steve eventually won last year. I have been on the Cannon and Ball Show and Tis Wos, the children's show, with Isla St Clair. In fact, I have done quite a few of the Saturday morning programmes. Question of Sport is another I have been on several times – and ITV's Sporting Triangles. I remember on the Cannon and Ball Show Sarah Brightman was singing. That was before she married Andrew Lloyd Webber and became a really big star. She used to be with Hot Gossip and when she sang I thought: What the hell's this?

I did a fair amount for Welsh television, of course, appearing on different sports shows and quiz programmes and also did something for the 1988 Telethon. I had to go to London to the Connaught Rooms where I met Norman Wisdom for the first time and Jim Davidson. The cast from the ITV series The Bill were there as well. I also went on TV AM when all the cameramen and technicians were on strike and the office staff ran the show. That was quite an experience, too!

One thing I have always found very strange and very glamorous was the photo sessions. And, of course, there were the records. Snooker Loopy got to number five in the charts and we made a video with Chas and Dave. That was done in Romford and what fun we had with it – one of the really enjoyable moments of my life. The Romford Rap was not nearly so successful and I thought it was a mistake. We should have lived on Snooker Loopy. After that, it was always going to be a flop. The video was better, but I do not think the song was as good.

It was interesting to see how they set up and filmed a video for a record. And I can always say I have been in the charts. How many people can claim that? And we appeared on Top of the Pops, although that was a recording. I often have a laugh when people ask me if I can sing, being a Welshman. I say, 'Well, I got to number five in the charts!' The Chicken Song was top at the time, I seem to remember.

It was all such a good experience, especially those photo sessions. There was one in London with an Aston Martin, where Steve, Tony and myself are in white dinner suits reflected on the bonnet.

My friend Alun was up with me at that session. He has been my best mate, really, and that goes back to the Welsh way of life, again. He and his wife Heather are our best friends. He is head mechanic in a garage and also has a smallholding. He always gives the impression of being a Welsh farmer, although he actually works in the garage most of the time.

On this occasion he had come to London with me – this was in the early Matchroom days – and we had hired the Aston Martin, which cost a cool £66,000, for the session. It turned out to be one of the best photographs we ever had taken. Now Alun has got an old A35 van – a 1957 model – which he chugs round the village in and uses to go and see his cows. You have to picture him, now, a typical dry Welsh character, and short, who has a knack of staying very serious when he is telling a joke.

The garage would not let the car out for the day unless the salesman came with it. So there was this guy in his pinstripe suit sitting in the studio. I watched Alun go up to him and I knew what he was up to. He was going to pull his leg, for sure. Anyway, he said to the salesman, 'Good God, what a super car.' It had all these gadgets and electronic things and Alun wanted to know all about it. And he eventually got every bit of information possible out of the salesman, who by now thought he must be on a sale. He naturally assumed that because Alun was with us, money was not a problem.

After about half an hour of going through every inch of the car, Alun said, 'I don't suppose you would take part exchange?' And I knew what was coming. Eagerly, the chap said, 'Yes, of course. What have you got?' So, all seriously, Alun replied, 'A 1957 Austin A35 van.' You should have seen the salesman's face. It was an absolute picture.

The first time the four of us went away together was to London for the weekend. Now Alun is a short dumpy character and we were walking down Piccadilly with all the traffic and the pavements jammed up with people. And there was Alun, bouncing backwards and forwards and side-stepping everyone all the way. The rest of us could not stop laughing.

When we were on holiday in Miami, we were trying to negotiate

International Drive, which is an infamous road – four lanes both ways – and you just cannot get across. Our two families were waiting patiently for a break in the traffic and there was a coloured family with us, too. So Alun decided he had had enough and walked into the middle of the road to stop the cars. He stood there with his arm up and waved us across, while all these drivers had screeched to a halt and were leaning on their horns. You can imagine the bedlam that caused.

Those types of incidents are very special. Everyone loves Alun; he's just one of those characters. If you get in a car with him, by the time you have gone a mile you feel you have known him twenty years. And then, after a while, he will turn to you and say, 'I'm getting to know you a bit, now.'

Our first big holiday as a family was in 1980, when I went to play in Canada at the CNE. We took the boys with us and had a tremendous time and saw Niagara Falls, although I think Wayne and Darren enjoyed the funfair most. One thing that sticks out about that holiday more than anything else is that they both learnt to swim on the trip. We were staying in a hotel with a swimming pool and the lads went down there as much as they could. One morning they insisted on taking me down to the pool and jumped straight in from the side. I had such a fright because I knew they could not swim before we arrived. It was a great thrill to think they had learnt on their own while we were there.

Strangely I had always been totally opposed to holidays. I had never liked them very much. But in the January before Canada, Annette and I went to Tenerife by ourselves. That week showed me how important a holiday was. I realised then that I needed time away from the snooker circuit. It was one of the few occasions Annette and I had spent alone for a long time and it totally changed my opinion of holidays.

We used to go with the boys to Pontins every year, where I would play as well. Then we decided with Dennis Taylor, Doug Mountjoy and their families – thirteen of us altogether – to go to Miami. Basically we had won enough Pontinental holiday vouchers through the snooker to take us there. It was a fabulous experience not only for the kids but us adults as well to see Disneyworld and all the other attractions.

A lot of funny things happened to us during that holiday.

174

Obviously nobody out there recognised us, so we used to go round in shorts and T-shirts. When we went to book in at our hotel it was so awful that Dennis and I decided to go and look for another better one. We went into this particular hotel down the road and asked: 'Is it possible to have a look at your suites?' The manager stared at us. There we were in shorts and looking a right mess. He must have wondered who the hell we were. It was the Holiday Inn. Surprisingly we did get booked in.

We did have a few ups and downs because there were so many of us and it was very difficult for everyone to agree on what to do or equally to do the same thing. But we had lots of fun, nevertheless. There was a bus called The Rabbit which used to pick you up from your hotel and take you out to the funfair or wherever you wanted to go. We could never take it because there were thirteen of us and by the time it had called at all the other hotels there were never any seats left.

Dennis started going out jogging, but he did not realise how hot it was. When he came back, he was so hot he could not cool down. Because he burns easily, he was red in the face and looked like a lobster for two days.

The irony of all this was that, deep down, the boys really loved Pontins because there they were let loose. And the following year, when we asked them where they wanted to go, they both picked Pontins, even though they could have gone anywhere they wanted.

As I have mentioned, we went back to Miami with Alun and Heather and their two children, Lorraine and Jason, in 1986. The Epcott Centre was open then. What a futuristic place that was, quite different from Disneyworld, although it was fascinating to see as well. During that holiday I had the misfortune to lose Annette's wallet with all her credit cards inside. So she would not give me any money to spend after that.

As far as I was concerned, the best part of Florida was the Wet and Wild, where there are water shoots and all sorts of different things going on in the water. They also have a machine that creates the most enormous waves. The first year we were there, Darren almost drowned and I shall never forget the look on his face as long as I live. I was standing at the side of the pool when the waves started. It was lucky I was there, otherwise he would have had it. The lifeguard was standing directly above him looking out at the mass of people in the water. I could see Darren and realised he just could not handle the waves which were crashing him into the side. I jumped in to get him and even I had a job to pull him out. It was a horrible experience.

For the last couple of years Annette and I have gone on our own to Puerto Rico, where there is sunshine 350 days of the year. It's very quiet and just the type of place where you can be alone and do exactly what you please.

Apart from being able to holiday where and when we like, snooker permitting, financial security has also enabled me to indulge one of my great fantasies – the motor car. I have always been a car freak and changed them as often as I could to get a better one – at least once a year and often twice. Of course in the early days, before I turned professional, money was very tight and I had to persuade Annette to let me spend some on another car, although usually it was more than we could afford.

But after 1979 I was obviously in a position to buy better cars and I certainly made the most of the opportunity. Over the years since, I have had four Mercedes and been through the full range of BMWs and Jaguars.

Now I am running Citroens. This came about in 1987 when Colin Bliss, who owns Highway Garage in Llandysul, asked me if I would put on an exhibition to open his new car showroom. When we worked out my fee and the expenses involved, rather than pay me we agreed that Colin would supply me with a car instead. I had a look at the range and chose a CX 2.5 GTI Turbo.

The arrangement has worked out very well on both sides. I did a television commercial for him as well as some local publicity and the following year Dennis Taylor and I put on another show at the garage. I am on my fourth Citroen now and Wayne, who also got a car, is on his third. The garage has gone from strength to strength and I like to think that my endorsement has helped in some way.

So, all in all, it is not a bad life being a snooker player. And one of the great things about having that kind of money is that I was able to share so much more of it with the family.

20 Players and Me

GENERALLY I LIKE to feel I get on well with my fellow players. It is a known fact that we tend not to mix much socially, although on the circuit we inevitably see a lot of each other. Apart from one or two brushes, particularly with Alex Higgins, which I have already mentioned, my matches have usually been played without incident. There was, of course, one exception, which happened at the beginning of this year.

I was playing Silvino Francisco in the first round of the Benson and Hedges Masters at the Wembley Conference Centre, when suggestions were made that our game had been fixed. The result was 5–1 in my favour and I found it a very hard, long match – very tough. When we finished, all of a sudden there was talk about a lot of heavy bets being put on for that result – 5–1 to me. Of course, I knew nothing about this until after the match.

Unfortunately, Silvino had been involved before, in a match with Tony Knowles – again in the Benson and Hedges, when a lot of money was put on a frame score that turned out to be correct. This time some betting shops, particularly in Ireland, had taken so many heavy bets at the correct score that they refused to take any more and asked the WPBSA to investigate.

Silvino was very upset about it. To me, he certainly tried very hard during the match. Despite that, I was close to winning 5–0. Having said that, I could have lost one or two more frames as well. But to me, the match itself did not bear out the stories carried in the newspapers the next day. But because Silvino had been involved before, the finger was pointing directly at him. I had won, so there was no way I could have fixed the result. It is always the loser who gets implicated.

The next day the television boys were in the hotel, with cameras pointing in my face as soon as I walked into the lounge – ironically for a meeting about this book. I said a few choice words to the reporter and then the Daily Mirror chap came up with his side-kick. Although I told him to f . . . off, he said he would take my picture anyway. It was all very upsetting at the time.

I cannot believe the fixing of matches happens. The amount of money that was put on in bets would not warrant Silvino being involved in it. If it ran to hundreds of thousands of pounds, possibly I could understand. But they were talking about small amounts of money. He was better off winning the match, since he would have got £13,000.

It created a lot of bad publicity on the television and in the newspapers and I got a bit of flack for it simply because I was there. I was disgusted by it all – and felt sorry for Silvino. There was an inquiry into the alleged incident. The last time this happened, the conclusion was that the allegations were unfounded, which I believe will be the result again.

I do not really know, deep down, how much it is to do with Silvino. Some people do not like him, possibly because he is South African. I do not think it could happen just like that. It is too much of a coincidence. I think there had to be somebody behind it. I do not understand why it had to be Ireland, either.

But looking at it from a totally innocent point of view, there are plenty of gamblers at snooker and it was a fair bet – 5–1 – because they were offering odds of 6–1 for me to win by that score and Silvino had not been playing very well. So it looked as though I would win the match and 5–1 or 5–2 was the sort of result many would have expected. Even if there were people trying to make a fuss about it, you would still have had plenty of ordinary punters wanting to put that bet on.

There was a further incident with Silvino and his nephew Peter. You see, it always seems to be Silvino. To me, if someone was trying to fix matches, they would be doing it with different players. When it is always Silvino, it looks too much of a coincidence. It had happened to a South African in Ireland. There are just too many odd things there for it to be true.

Apart from anything else, I do not know of any snooker player who could live with himself or ever play again if he ever tried to lose on purpose for money. It is like a boxer lying down. I suppose it has been done, but I do not see how they could ever get up and box again. I just cannot see Silvino doing it – or any other player, come to that. I cannot believe anyone would have that lack of faith in themselves to want to be beaten. Otherwise, you could never compete again. Playing is all about self-belief.

There have been happier, less controversial moments in the game over the last year or so – and none more than the return to form of Doug Mountjoy. My relationship with Doug goes back to the early Seventies, when we were both amateurs. We played a lot of games together, had many battles on the table, represented our country together and got to know each other quite well. We used to spend time in each other's homes and our wives got to know each other too. There was the trip to Johannesburg when Doug won the World Amateur title and it was a particularly nice gesture on his part to allow Annette to share the Pontins holiday he won with his wife, because we were all skint at the time.

When I turned professional, Doug had already done so. We were then quite close because there were not so many competitions and we used to do a lot of exhibition work together. Doug was a very successful professional at that time. Then I came along and won the World Championship and had a lot of publicity over it. In the meantime, Doug suffered a few personal problems. His brother committed suicide, which affected him very badly, and then he had Bell's Palsy. I remember going to his house and seeing him. His face had dropped right down. He was in a terrible state about it, what with his eyes and everything, because it was obviously affecting his snooker. This was the mid-Eighties and his game was falling back.

I started the World Doubles with Doug as my partner and would normally never have left him. When I joined up with Barry Hearn, he wanted me to team up with one of the Matchroom players, if possible. There was also another, more important reason, however, for breaking the partnership.

At that time Doug had, as I said, gone through a bad slump. Now as a person he is the complete opposite to me – very quiet and withdrawn and unwilling to talk about personal matters. I, on the other hand, am quite open. I would phone Doug. He would never phone me. That was how it was. We were different people, but we had a good relationship. So when I decided to find another doubles partner, I wanted to tell Doug personally. We were due to play in Pot Black and I made up my mind to talk to him there rather than over the phone.

I did not like doing it, but the reason I did was that I had tried to help Doug in my own way, but had been rejected. I went up to his house a few times after he had had some bad results. His wife Yvonne had asked me, 'For God's sake, can you do anything with Doug? His form has gone and he's so miserable.'

Apart from the technical side of the game, which I knew a bit more about than Doug because I had spent a lot of time studying it, at least I felt I was somebody who would sit there and talk on the same level about the mental side of snooker. You cannot talk about that with anyone else, because they have not competed. The problem was that I would chat to him in the hope that I could help, because he had helped me so much when I started off, but there was no response.

I tried in my own way quite a few times. But Doug was a very proud person and really he was not willing to accept advice from me. I found that quite hurtful, really, as I did watching Doug play so badly when I knew what a good player he really was. So that was the main reason why I did not want to play with him in the doubles anymore. It got to the stage when it was affecting me when I was playing him. I was not getting good results against him because of all these circumstances.

After all this, I found out that Doug had said a few other things that he had not said to me. Up at Pontins he claimed I had dropped him because he was not playing very well. Now I would never have done it for that reason. I would always have stuck by him. And that hurt badly. It was made worse because he did not tell me to my face. I had to hear it from others.

The next time I saw Doug after this was in Hong Kong during a tour, when he was invited out to the Far East with us. I had finished with him in the doubles the previous Christmas. Since then we had drifted apart quite a bit and had not kept in touch. I took the opportunity to bring everything out into the open and explained my situation to him. In turn, he explained his and said he felt I had dropped him because he had been playing badly, which just was not true. Then he said something that really hit home, 'Well, I wouldn't care how badly you were playing, I would never have finished with you.'

Since that day we have always got on well. Up until then we had gone through a patch where we did not really communicate with one another. And when I joined up with Barry I had drifted away a bit and had always felt he resented that a little – not me personally – but more the publicity I had got through it. But then, I had a different personality to him.

Anyway, Doug's game was getting worse and worse, until it got to the stage in 1987 when he reached an all-time low. I stopped watching in the end because I found it so hurtful to see him lose to players he could have given a 50 start to. Then I urged him to go and see Frank Callan, which he did – before the World Team Championship in March 1988. From my point of view that was a disaster, because he came to that tournament trying out a new technique, which always takes ages to perfect. I was talking to him recently and recalled the night he was practising with me before the match. I always remember thinking: Bloody hell, we've had it for the world team now. And I wrote Doug off because I have been through all that to and know what it does to your game.

So what Doug did, which is what he has always done because he works as hard as anyone I know and has always been a totally dedicated player, was to work on what Frank had told him during that summer. He went up to see Frank a few more times and, of course, started off the 1988/89 season with much better results.

In the UK championship in Preston, he played as good snooker as I have ever seen him play, including a good thrashing for yours truly. Doug beat me 9–4 in the semi-final and totally outplayed me. He met Hendry in the final, who had beaten Steve Davis easily in the other semi. Everyone said, 'Well, that's it, Hendry will win.' But I thought if Doug played as he did against me, then Hendry had got one hell of a fight on his hands. It was just whether Doug had the confidence in himself, because he had had so many years of defeat. I believed he now had that confidence to win because certainly his game was good enough. He proved everyone wrong and played as good snooker as anyone has ever played in a final – including three consecutive centuries – and beat an in-form Stephen Hendry quite comfortably. Then he went to the Mercantile Credit and won that. So he had won two tournaments back-to-back.

I played Doug again in the final of the Welsh Professional in February this year. I was 5–2 in front, although I was not doing anything special, but that should have been enough to win, because it was the first to nine. Then in the evening session Doug came out and beat me 7–1. And he played probably the best snooker I have ever had played against me. He won six of those frames with one scoring visit to the table each time, including breaks of 124, 90, two 80s and a 70. That one chance in each game had gone and no-one has ever scored that heavily against me before in an important final – and from behind, as well. I just did not get a chance to play. I said afterwards in my speech that the quality of Doug's snooker was as good as I have ever had played against me.

About two years ago Doug was really in the pits. He could not do anything. And to see him now is an object lesson to anybody. If you have got the will and determination and are prepared to put in the work day in and day out throughout the summer when you are really on a low and you have got the skill, which obviously Doug had, and you are willing to forget about your pride and ask someone for help, which he did with Frank Callan, then you can do it.

At forty-six years of age, Doug has been a breath of fresh air in the game – as much as Stephen Hendry or Jimmy White in the last few years. There are so many players who think they are past it at thirty-five. But seeing a player like Doug do that gives everybody fresh hope. His achievement last year was as big as anything that has ever been done in snooker. When you get as low as he did, even winning a match is so difficult. Winning a tournament is an impossibility. Because your confidence is so low, even if you are playing well you do not believe you can win. And he has overcome all that through hard work, self-belief and putting pride out of the way and asking for help. It all worked for him and that is great. I think everybody in the snooker world was pleased.

In direct contrast, there is Stephen Hendry. I first saw him on Junior Pot Black some years ago. He was so young at the time and he told me later he was almost crying when he lost to Steve Ventham, who made a 60 break to beat him in the semi-final, after he had made a 50. He was then about twelve or thirteen, but actually looked eight or nine. I remember thinking how great it was to see somebody so young playing so well.

I met him afterwards on the amateur circuit at Pontins and other places and again in Dublin at the final of the World Amateur Championship. There he was with his dad, as always, very well dressed and very well behaved. He had not made a big impression on the tournament, but he had certainly made a big impression on me.

Even though he had lost in an earlier round, he had stayed on to watch. He was willing to learn. All these things stuck out to me. If the boy had talent as well, I knew he could make the grade.

Then, all of a sudden, professional status came his way. I watched him play a few times and one thing I noticed more than anything was that he was what I call a wild sort of player. He played all the shots. If they went in, it was great; if they did not, then he would lose. He was young and I thought: Why not? And, what to me is the most important thing, when he was really up against it, he always came on strong. I knew then that the boy was going to be a handful, if he got himself together.

I remember, too, watching him in the World Doubles at the Derngate Centre in Northampton, which he won with Mike Hallett. He actually influenced my thinking about playing the game. He was going for the most ridiculous shots and getting them and it was so refreshing. I thought: Christ, nobody's playing like that on the circuit, because it is all too tense. But this kid was in and he was going for everything. He did not care. It was so good to watch. And I thought to myself: What the hell am I playing all this safety for? I can play those shots. I can express myself playing snooker and I have not done it for years. And it took someone like Stephen Hendry, watching him play even before he won a title, to make me realise possibly some of the faults I had got in myself. That is why I have always enjoyed watching snooker because I find you can always learn something from other players.

Anyway Stephen has gone on from there and is now a major force. He has won quite a few events and undoubtedly he is going to be the number one player in the world in the future.

He came down and played a show in my club recently, which was nice. His manager Ian Doyle said he would like to come down when I had opened the club, which he did free of charge. He played exceptionally well, but more important than that he was so good afterwards, so professional, and that has a lot to do with Ian, of course. He has groomed him very well.

Ian told me, 'Stephen wants to come down and play because you were one of the first people to talk to him on the professional circuit.' I do not do it for any particular reason; I just enjoy talking to people. But for Stephen at the time, when he had just started off, it was very important because, although I was one of the senior players, I had bothered to ask him how he was playing. That stuck in the kid's mind.

Now Stephen is undoubtedly the best potter in the game. He is a phenomenal potter of the ball, quite frightening – and again, totally dedicated, unbelievably professional for a young player and straight as a die. He never steps out of line. For a youngster with all the publicity and success he has had, that takes some doing. But he has not changed at all.

He is probably not the perfect example for other youngsters simply for the way he plays the game, because he plays very much his own style. But in every other respect he is the perfect professional – and how often can you say that of a young kid? But he is. He has got the skill and now he has got the bottle as well. And he will be the number one, the world champion, in my opinion. He has got to be.

Another player who impresses me enormously is John Parrott, who also goes to Frank Callan for coaching. I remember watching John play back in the early Eighties when he turned professional and beat Alex Higgins 5–1 at the Spectrum Arena in Warrington. That was one of his first matches and he played tremendously well. I thought then he was going to be good. John always had the appearance; he looked the part of the professional – tall, elegant, always immaculately turned out and very keen. Of course, he won Junior Pot Black. I saw him on that and also at Pontins, when he beat Ray Reardon in the final, which was quite an occasion for him.

But quite honestly John was until recently a big disappointment. He just had not done what I thought he would. In the last season or two, however, he has finally blossomed and got through to quite a few major finals – and is currently one of the top four players in the world. He beat me in the European Open final in Deauville in February this year, his first major ranking tournament success, although he has won some smaller events.

In getting to so many finals and playing so consistently well, it was only a matter of time before he did win his first title. The only problem was that I was on the receiving end. We had a long, hard match in which there was quite a lot of good snooker – and some bad as well. It all came down to the final frame and he took it pretty comfortably to win 9–8.

I have to say I got a lot of pleasure out of seeing him win his first major tournament. I would have preferred to have won it myself, of course, but it did not stop me feeling how good it was for him. I spoke to his father afterwards on the phone from the press room. That was quite funny. His dad is a real character and I said to him, 'Congratulations. Did John tell you about the fourteen flukes he had in the first frame?' His dad replied, 'I don't care how many flukes he had, as long as he won.' I then said, 'You should be very proud of him.' I knew he was. I could feel it, even over the phone.

I have always liked the way John plays the game. I will go so far as to say that there have been times when I would like to be able to hit the ball the way he does. I have always thought he was a bit open as a player, but in the last few seasons, particularly last year, he has added safety to his obvious potting game and that is why he has been more successful. Now he is a very dangerous opponent for everybody.

Looking back over the years in the game, both as an amateur and a professional, there are several players I have admired, for various reasons. One of those was John Spencer, a tremendous player, with great cue power. He had such an easy-going, relaxed way of playing the game that just made you relax watching. He was one of those players who made you want him to get every ball – so smooth and elegant.

Sadly John lost his game somewhere in the Eighties. I played him a lot and inflicted a few bad defeats. He led me 4–2 in the Benson and Hedges on one occasion and I beat him 5–4. There was a similar score in a Jameson International match. Both those he should have won. But he never said anything. He was the best player in the world on his way down, from my point of view, but he never said a word out of place. He always accepted his defeats gracefully, shook your hand and said 'well done'. I have always remembered John for that. Some players have said he was not a very good loser, but to me he has always been the model player, always the perfect gentleman, and he has never said anything bad in the press. If I have to remember one thing about John, it would be the way he used to move the white ball. He had this wonderful knack – tremendous power, so graceful and so much touch.

As an amateur, my real idol was Ray Reardon – for his balance of play, his tactics and, more than anything else, his overwhelming personality. You could feel it when you were watching and I used to feel it when I played him. When he came down to play exhibitions locally, I used to look forward to that. For me, it was the highlight of

185

the year. To play a frame against Ray was tremendous. But for some reason there was always a clash between Ray and myself.

I recall one incident, back in 1975, when Ray had finished an exhibition and we were chatting afterwards. At that time I was beginning to make my name as an amateur. Ray, who was always a straightforward, direct person, said to me: 'How do you fancy touring South Africa with me?' I was stunned. I went back home that night and told Annette I was going to South Africa. I even started making arrangements. In the meantime, I never heard any more from him. I realise now I should have rung him up. The next time I saw him, nothing was said and I thought it had just been cancelled. I met Ray the following year at Pontins and I went up and shook his hand. 'How's it going?' I asked. He replied, 'Oh, are you still playing then?' I thought: What's he saying that for? Then I realised that I had never said I was going to South Africa. I assumed he had taken it for granted. But he must have thought I had ignored him. It was simply a misunderstanding, but perhaps he took it the wrong way.

After I won the World Championship, I played Ray a few times in exhibitions. On one occasion, when I beat him, he said to someone standing nearby, 'He's just trying to knock me off the table. He's going for everything.' Now for a man I idolised, I felt very insulted. He never summed me up properly. He also said a few things in the press about my joining up with Barry and about the way I played, which I felt were out of place.

In the early days he used to have Doug up to his house and they arranged shows together. He never did that with me. Unfortunately he is not that popular among other players as a person because he has always been of the opinion that you should never make friends on the circuit. I think he has a point, and he has always kept to that and distanced himself from other professionals.

On the positive side, Ray carried the game through the Seventies and was a very good ambassador for the sport. But I have also witnessed a lot of unfortunate incidents, when he has said things out of place to people. Now, perhaps I can understand why to a degree, because I know what it is like being on the circuit all the time. But then I found it hard to accept why he was telling people off and causing unnecessary aggravation.

Ray was notorious for knocking referees down and stamping his authority on proceedings. On this particular occasion, I was playing him at Pontins. He was world champion at the time and I had won the English Amateur title. The thrill of playing him in a match was so much for me. He beat me 4–1 and I was lucky to win the one frame. He certainly gave me a lesson in snooker that day, but not one I particularly want to remember. The referee had made a mistake and Ray shouted at him across the table in front of 1000 people, 'If you can't do your job properly, get off.' He humiliated that man and I did not feel he had any right to do that. Then he turned round to the crowd and said, 'Red'. He tried to make a joke of it, but the damage had been done. He was too big a man to have to do that. The incident did not overwhelm me; he had already done that with his play. But there was an arrogance he had to bring out.

There was another occasion at Pontins, which involved Des Magness, a friend of mine from Merthyr. It was his first time as a referee at Pontins, so you can imagine how he was feeling. Ray was playing an amateur from London called Roy Conner. I had been knocked out and was watching the match, which was being played on one of the corner tables. There were loads of people around and plenty of hustle and bustle. Des was introducing the players to the crowd and tried to build it up a bit, 'Roy Conner, who's the London and Home Counties champion, against the one and only Ray Reardon.' Everyone clapped and then Ray said, 'From nowhere.' Now Des had gone – and the match had not even started. I thought: What did you do that for?

Ray had by now got it in mind to do the referee in. There were rows of seats round the table all locked together and he said to Des, 'I'm not having this. Get these chairs moved.' Des panicked and grabbed the first chair. Of course, he could not move it because it was attached to at least twenty or so others in the row. I was sitting there thinking: Get on with the game, man. Then Ray decided he wanted the long rest and there was not one there. So Des went off through the crowd to four or five other tables looking for one, without any luck. He came back. 'Sorry, I can't find one.' So Ray said, 'There's plenty downstairs. We'll wait while you get one.'

That's why I could never understand Ray. He beat the amateur 4–0 and there was only ever going to be one result. He was good enough not to have to put the opposition off. But I believe he was doing it just for that reason.

Steve Davis had a similar problem when he played Ray in Ipswich

187

once. Ray had the referee set up the triangle four times. Steve could not understand what was going on and lost 4–0. But I am sure it was all down to gamesmanship.

I shall never forget Ray's reaction when I put on that trick shot exhibition at the Sports Review of the Year show in 1979. I came off the table feeling quite thrilled and sat down. Ray was next to me and if only he had turned round and just said, 'Well done.' But he did not say a word. So many others came up and said, 'Well done, Terry.' They realised it was difficult for me. But I think the jealousy factor was there. We all went for a meal afterwards and, would you believe it, Ray actually sent the potatoes back. What a strange man, a strange character – and a Welshman through and through.

I spoke up against Ray at an AGM once and I do not think he was very keen on that, either. He looked on me as a young whipper-snapper coming through who had only just won the world title. Up till then, Ray had dominated the committee meetings. IMG was making its initial approach to the governing body and I was in the chair that day. Mark McCormack's representative put forward a proposal and Ray stood up and absolutely slated the fellow. I had to apologise and explain it was just Ray's point of view. 'What do these people want?' he kept saying. 'Why are they coming here asking for all this money? We're doing alright ourselves.' The man always had to stamp his authority wherever he went, which I always thought was a great weakness in his make-up.

Now he is a shadow of his former self and I find it very difficult to watch him play anymore. It is a shame, really, seeing him as a fallen idol. He has always given me help when I have asked him, although it has been a genuine help that was very cold.

I used to believe Ray was the best ever but now I think Steve is. They both have similar talent on the table. But whereas Ray had the advantage of overwhelming players with his very strong personality, Steve has never had this. He has had to do it all with his cue. And that to me is the greater achievement.

Having said all that, I still have enormous respect for Ray as a player, as was highlighted at the World Team Championship in 1986. His game had been drifting off and he was having problems at home, as well. His eyes were giving him trouble and, to cap it all, he had lost his cue. There we were – Ray, Doug and myself – and we had been playing together since 1979. We were in the dressing room after Ray had just lost and he said, 'Never mind, you won't have to put up with me next year. You'll be better off without me.' That went through me like a knife. He said it for the right reasons but it was the wrong thing to say. I told him I would rather have him in the team anyday – and I meant it.

Without doubt the greatest single influence on my career as a professional has been the master himself – Steve Davis. Steve has gone right through – from my late amateur days to the present.

He was very quiet in those early years. I remember one occasion which typifies this. We were doing a tour together and had played Potters in Manchester where he beat me 5–2. Then we travelled to Louth and I turned the tables on him up there. After the match we went for a Chinese meal and during the evening I asked him how his game was going. He refused to talk about it. There were other occasions, for example when I won the English Amateur Championship and later when I was thrashed by Rex Williams in my first professional game. Steve watched both matches, but never said anything to me afterwards.

Of course, I played him in my defence of the world title in 1980. I had watched him play the year before against Dennis Taylor – a marvellous match which he just lost 13–11. I was very impressed, particularly by the way he fought back so hard. When he beat me in that first round, he got some bad publicity for it. I felt sorry for him. He had gone 7–1 up in the first session and did a television interview. It was a very arrogant interview and I do not think he took into account he was playing the defending champion, whom everyone wanted to win. He said things like, 'I could see Terry was very nervous in his chair and I knew I could give him a beating.' It did not offend me, because I knew Steve and understood why he was saying it. But it did upset a lot of people who watched it. He started off badly as far as image was concerned and I know found it difficult to put it right, which of course he has now done.

That was a tremendous match. I came back to 10–10 before he beat me 13–10. The game had everything – defending champion against the new youngster. I never had a chance to see him afterwards to wish him luck in the rest of the tournament, so dropped him a note instead. He could not believe that. But that is why I have always got on so well with Steve, because we were such different characters doing the same thing.

For Steve, that was the start. He got public exposure. Later that year he won the UK for the first time, where he beat me 9–0 in the semi-final – my first-ever whitewash! It was a fair result. Mentally I was in a bad way and Steve played brilliantly. He then beat Higgins in the final. That really launched him. I remember ringing Barry afterwards to give him some advice! I told him he should put Steve's fee up a lot. When I look back, it was very funny; there was me trying to tell Barry what to do. Typically, Barry had replied, 'I already have'.

Steve's reign started at that time. Generally I was playing pretty well, but everytime we came up against each other, it seemed he was beating me. Mind you, he was beating everyone else as well. I had a few successes against him in the early period, but very few. That was really what made me stop and analyse my game, which as events proved put my game in the doldrums for several years.

Over the years, Steve and I have become good friends. Now I would ask Steve for advice about my game, which I do not think any other player would – and equally I do not think Steve would offer it to any other player – very few anyway. Ironically, considering the titles he has 'robbed' me of, I am one of the few players who really wants to see him win, because I have got so much respect for him both on and off the table. And through the early Eighties I defended him against a lot of criticism. I suppose that goes back to the image he inadvertently created, which was totally out of character. I think Barry blended that into him. He created an image and to be fair he did well. But what really matters is his play – and that is phenomenal. I have never seen anyone play like him. His achievements are just incredible. No-one as ever played the game consistently to the standard Steve has.

We have spent a lot of time on tours together and Steve has softened up a lot. He has also become a model professional. In fact, off the table he is so bloody professional, sometimes it is sickening. He is never late, always dresses properly, always says the right thing. He never criticises an opponent. He never seems to do anything wrong in public. Sometimes I just cannot understand why he has not cracked up. Sooner or later you have got to do something wrong, but he never does. He has had his bad spells by his own standards, but even then I have never heard him say anything about the other player – he was lucky or he was this or that, which all the other players tend to do.

There was one incident, a few years back, when I played him in Belgium straight after my summer holidays. I had not touched a cue for a fortnight and really should have had no chance. Yet I beat Steve 5–2 and went on to win the tournament. To be fair, Steve did not play very well. Several reporters were waiting when he emerged from the dressing room and he said, 'I played like a bloody idiot.' He realised what he had said and thought that was taking it away from my victory. It did not worry me. He was right. He did play badly. But even though he was mad at losing, he just could not say something that might upset his opponent.

Even off the table, we have rarely had reason to clash, although there was one occasion when I spoke my mind about Steve, which I confess was how I felt at the time but should have been more diplomatic.

Barry had agreed a snooker v pool challenge in Dallas and, according to him, we were going to blaze a trail across America promoting snooker. By this stage, Steve had really hit the big time. He was everywhere and on everything. Anyway, we arrived at this hotel in Dallas ready to show the Yanks what the game was all about. The place had a skating rink with a large cover over it – and that was where we were going to play! As it turned out, it was a catastrophe. There is no other word for it.

That day had not gone too well. I decided to have a go about Steve's fee. We were sitting in the hotel waiting for Steve and I was getting more and more hungry. 'Wait until Steve comes down and we'll go and eat together,' said Barry.

Two hours later Steve had not appeared. So I said, 'Well, are we going to wait for this guy or not. Just because he's world champion, he can command what fees he likes. But it doesn't entitle him to be a cunt.'

As soon as I had said it, I knew it was wrong. We were in company and I should have kept the remark until Barry and I were on our own. But at that time I did mean it.

Looking back now, the whole affair was actually quite hilarious. The challenge had been fixed up by Richard Town, the chap from Stoke I had talked to before about managing my affairs. Barry had got together with him because Richard had a few contacts in the States and they had got a sponsor. The first night was the snooker and Richard had told us there had been a tremendous response. About 1000 people were coming.

The event was due to start at 7.30 and at 7.15 I heard a noise outside my bedroom window, which overlooked the skating rink. I had a peep out and could not believe it. They still had not put any seats up and the table was only half finished. I thought: This is strange. When's everyone coming and where are they going to sit? By the time the match started – about 8.15 – somehow or other they had got some seats up. There was coconut matting over the ice, which meant our feet were bloody freezing. And, as I expected, virtually nobody came to watch – after we had travelled all that way.

Since snooker was new to America, we obviously tried to attract as much publicity as possible. So we had arranged a meeting with the Dallas Cowboys on their training ground, along with a few press boys. As soon as Barry, Steve and myself arrived, we knew they did not want to know. There were a few reserve players hanging about who could not get into the team and they were roped in for the photographs. I always remember standing alongside this 6ft 9in American footballer whom nobody had ever heard of and we all realised it was just not going to happen.

This was followed by a local radio station that apparently wanted to do an interview with us. It had been arranged for about 8.30 in the morning – and live. The only trouble was the studio was some thirty miles from the hotel. Barry had tried to muster up some enthusiasm, 'Come on lads, we've got to go to this interview and get some interest in the event.' So we got into the limousine Barry had ordered and drove for about three-quarters of an hour to the studio. I thought: Jesus, what are we doing this for? Anyway, Steve and Barry had a few words in the car on the way over. I had never heard them arguing before. It was not a quarrel, but they said some bad things that really hurt. They were giving each other a lot of stick.

Eventually we arrived and walked in. The woman in reception asked us to wait while she made a call. She spoke to someone and then said, 'I'm sorry but there's no-one to see you.' It was so funny. Here was Steve, the biggest name in snooker whom any television channel in this country would have given anything to get an interview with. And we had travelled all this way first thing in the morning to a little radio station in the outback and they had virtually told us to piss off.

We had plenty of laughs about it afterwards, but it just about summed up the whole visit. Even pool was not that highly regarded in

America and certainly the pool players did not want to know us. We have not been back there since and I do not think that situation is ever going to change. America is a dead loss as far as snooker is concerned.

When it comes to the game itself, Steve is as good a mate as I could ever get, although we are in many ways very distant. We both have our own lives to lead, but we will always be friends both on and off the table. We have had so many great battles together over the years that we have come to cement a relationship out of them. In all these years I have never slagged him off as far as the game is concerned. Players have given him a bad press because he was beating them all the time, but I have just accepted it. We have never really had any bad words together. Steve would not anyway. He would rather walk away, because he does not like confrontation – except, of course, on the table.

He did say something to me once which he immediately drew back on. We were having a bit of fun over his playing and I was giving him some stick after he had lost a match. He retorted, 'Well, I've never had any trouble beating you.' As soon as it came out, he realised he should not have said it.

We have shared a lot of laughs together, believe it or not even in that trouble-torn city of Belfast, where Steve and I were playing in the Northern Ireland Classic in 1982. The promoter had asked us if we would pay a visit to one of the hospitals between sessions. The schedule was very tight, particularly since the afternoon frames took a bit longer than normal. We rushed off to the hospital, which was supposed to be a quarter of an hour away but inevitably was nearer an hour, and went round a few of the wards.

There were elderly people in one particular ward and the sister took us over to see this chap, who was actually sleeping at the time. She woke him up, which could not have pleased him too much, and said, 'Look who's come to see you.' All drowsy and drugged up, he said, 'Who is it?' 'Steve Davis.' Now Steve had just lost 10–1 to Tony Knowles in the World Championship and the chap said, 'You're not doing very bloody well at the moment are you?' Poor Steve. He had gone in to brighten up the patients and there was this chap having a go at him.

On the way back, we were laughing about this and Steve said to me, 'Do you know, I really felt like saying to that chap – I'm doing a lot better that you are, by the looks of things!'

193

I shall never forget one visit I made to Northern Ireland, this time with Dennis Taylor. He had invited me over to his local club and inevitably I was asked to do some trick shots. I suppose I was pushing my luck a little, but I put that down to the Welsh sense of humour, when I finished my programme with the machine gun shot where you lay the white towards the corner pocket and fire in a row of reds before it gets there. Having set it all up, I told the audience what this trick was to be, adding, 'The only trouble is I haven't got a machine gun.' A voice from the back of the room called out, 'Don't you worry, Terry. We can soon fix that up for you!' Needless to say, I did not wait.

On that trip Dennis took me into Belfast because I wanted to see for myself how bad the trouble there really was. In fact, you often find you are pleasantly surprised because fortunately you rarely see anything going on. I remember passing a Burton's shop and stopping to look at the clothes in the window. After a while, Dennis pipes up, 'Don't be nervous just because that dummy over there is wearing a bullet-proof vest. Don't let it put you off!' I grabbed his arm and pulled him back down the street to the car.

Our Far East tours always coincide with Steve's birthday. One year we were staying in a hotel in Singapore and were waiting to go off to a reception. Steve was the last one down and eventually emerged from the lift, which was right the other side from where we were sitting in this vast reception area. As he stepped out, we all struck up a chorus of happy birthday. His face went bright red and he stormed over as if he was about to kill us all. That, however, is typical of the Romford humour. We do tend to take the piss out of each other, but it is usually all very harmless. If you react, you get more of the same, so you learn to take it.

I could not talk about Steve without mentioning his dedication, which is super-human and continuous. The way he has kept himself together through all he has been doing and still wants to win so much is phenomenal. He competes so hard all the time.

I remember playing him in a UK final and he was giving me a real hammering. In one frame I snookered him on the blue and he took ages working out how to get out of it. Finally he chose his shot and played it well. You should have seen the reaction on his face. It meant nothing to me because the match was really over and done with. But to him each shot is a challenge and always will be. He just keeps his level of competing constant all the time. I have not got it in me to do that – not everyday, every frame. And that, as much as anything else, is why he has been so successful. It is the ability to fight for every shot every day of the week – and enjoy it.

The best way to sum up Steve is through an incident that happened after I joined up with him and Tony. We were playing at the Brighton Conference Centre in a 17-frame match that Barry had promoted. We had to do a spot for the local radio and this interviewer was desperately trying to make something of the event. 'Well, Barry's promoting this so I suppose it will be 4–4 after the first eight frames.' Laughingly, Steve replied, 'I suppose so.' There was no point in saying anything else.

We went on to play and by the interval Steve was ahead 8–0! All he wanted was one frame in the evening and there were 1000 people packed in to watch. It looked a disaster. Steve had played magnificently in the afternoon. In the meantime, I was recalling the interview and thinking how funny it was. I actually won the first frame of the evening, then Steve took the next with an 80 break. We had only been playing half-an-hour and everyone was wondering what was going to happen. I called referee John Smythe over and said, 'Ask Steve if he wants to play the best of seven for £500 just to make some interest in the rest of the evening.' So John told Steve, who said, 'I don't mind what happens. I just want to win more frames.' I burst out laughing. Then he came over and we were both laughing. But what he said first, he really felt, although he saw the funny side of it. That is the man's will to win. He did not mean it against me in any way.

So we went on again and now I had got the hump. What a cheeky sod! I thought. I tried really hard and still lost.

Then we had another radio interview at the end. The guy realised that snooker was not about sharing frames. It may well have been in the very early days, but it is much too competitive now. Although people talk about fixed games, as with the Silvino affair, they should really relate to that incident, because at 8–0 there is no way it can happen.

What sadly does happen is players taking drugs, although as far as I am aware it is certainly not widespread. The sport has had some unfortunate – and in some cases, I believe, unnecessary – publicity over it. There was, for example, the incident some years ago when Silvino Francisco accused Kirk Stevens of taking drugs. Although this

195

was never proved at the time, ironically Kirk later admitted voluntarily that he was in the habit of taking drugs.

The whole question was thrown in front of the public when in the 1988 British Open Cliff Thorburn was the subject of the first positive drug test in the history of the game, not a record he would care to be reminded of too often. I personally think the idea of dope tests for players is sad. It makes you feel like a criminal whether you are guilty or not.

But what was particularly unfair, to my mind, was the fuss made of the use of Betablockers, which both Rex Williams and Neal Foulds admitted to taking. Although they affect the heart rate, I cannot believe that can be seriously compared to the range of drugs taken, for example, by athletes to boost performances.

If any general criticism had to be levelled in all this, then as far as I am concerned it should be at the WPBSA for the way in which it handled individual situations. Of course the governing body has to be seen to be doing the right thing for the sport, but I believe its actions should have been much more positive. Deducting two ranking points off Cliff Thorburn after his misdemeanour affected not just him but others as well – me, for example. As a result, it altered the seedings for the World Championship and gave me a much tougher draw than I would otherwise have had. If someone is guilty of a breach of the rules, it should not adversely affect other players, as this did. To my mind the punishment was obvious. He should have been stopped from playing straightaway, as should Alex Higgins for that matter, after that famous head-butting incident involving Paul Hatherell.

All this apart, however, snooker has as far as I am concerned survived its popularity remarkably well, considering the enormous pressures most of the top players are now under.

21 The Hardest Lesson

I REGARD THE snooker club and the new house very much as symbols of my achievement and success over the years. But as in all things, there is a price to pay. For me it has been the mental scars from the effort and time I put into both projects. They kept me away from the family and stole precious months I needed to relax and unwind. As in any business, you need a good break every so often. But because I chose to sacrifice that for two years, it did nothing to help my professional career. And what I tended to forget during that period was that snooker was my way of life, the way I earn money. I know now that I was very unwise to take on what I did with the club and the house. I should have had someone to do it for me. It may have cost more money, but after saying that it could have saved me a lot more on the circuit.

I started the 1987/88 season badly, despite the freakish run in the Laings, where I got to the final on the day we were opening the club doors. I made a fourth round exit in the Fidelity Unit Trusts International thanks to Eddie Charlton and lost in the fifth round of the Rothmans Grand Prix to John Parrott.

Then came a string of quarter-final defeats, first in the UK Open to Jimmy White. Neal Foulds and I were paired for the World Doubles and got to a similar stage, where we were comfortably disposed of by the eventual winners – Mike Hallett and Stephen Hendry. Steve Newbury pipped me by the odd frame in nine for a semi-final place in the Mercantile Credit Classic, while my 'old mate' Steve whitewashed me in the quarter-final of the Benson and Hedges Masters. And in the British Open Stephen Hendry brushed me aside in the fourth round on his way to the title.

By the end of the season, my snooker was coming together better and some of the old confidence was creeping back into my game. One of my most successful tournaments over the years has been the Benson and Hedges Irish Masters (there's Welsh for you!) and in 1988 I got as far as the semi-final, before being knocked out by Neal Foulds. I gained some consolation from scoring the highest break ever in the competition's history – 139. I also notched up my third Welsh title in four years by beating Wayne Jones 9–3 in the final, although I was given a nasty shock by Cliff Wilson in the previous match, when I won the last five frames after being 7–4 down.

Without doubt, however, the highlight of the season – and several seasons, for that matter – was making the final of the World Championship again – after nine years' absence. There is no need to guess who my opponent was. And at 8–8 overnight, I was in with every chance of winning that coveted title for the second time. Sadly the final day proved a real anti-climax. It was never a great game of snooker, but I made too many mistakes and you cannot afford to do that against the world number one. Steve eventually cruised home 18–11.

I am convinced that my performance at The Crucible was a direct result of my finally settling into the new club. For the first time in ages, I was feeling a lot happier with my game. It was the April after the club opened and I now had somewhere to play, somewhere to practise. At last I felt part of the place and was spurred on because I knew the boys in the club wanted me to win. I was playing more for them, really, and felt much closer to those people who wanted me to do well.

Professional sport is not only very demanding but can also be very destructive, particularly when you are always playing people of a consistently high standard. Only when I see younger players struggling away in the club do I ever remind myself of the talent I have. On the circuit it is very easy to forget that, because you are playing at that level all the time. It is only when you go back to the grass roots of the game and see how it is being played locally that you can put it all in perspective. I remember thinking after one match in the World Championship what a good player I was. Not that you thought about it during a match. You cannot when you are playing in the fiercely competitive world of professional snooker against players who are top of the tree all the time. But it can be a useful reminder when things are not going quite right – and that is where the club proved a great help mentally.

When you reach the very top, where you are among the best eight or ten players in the world, and you play against them continuously, it is always very misleading because there need not be anything wrong with your game, but you are just not getting the amount of chances you need to make your mark. When you watch the game afterwards, you can very often see that it was just the one or two missed chances that let your opponent in. If you had got another chance or two, which normally you would against lesser players, then the result could well have been very different. But that is what you have to live with when you get to the top. You are judged at the highest level.

There have been times in my career when I have performed very badly in tournaments and yet in practice have been playing very well. When you get up against the best players, the chances are fewer and, if your confidence is not at its peak, you can look as though you are bad. If I were up against an amateur player, I would look like the world champion. But you are not measured by amateurs. You are measured by other world champions and you have to accept that. You may lose every final you reach, but that does not mean you are not still one of the best players in the game. The standards now are very high indeed. And these are set by your fellow players – and Steve Davis more than anyone else.

My life for the last ten years or so has been snooker and my family. Nothing else. Everything has revolved around those two. I have never been the sort of person to go out on my own. I do not drink and so would not go to pubs. Now the club has given me a base. I have got somewhere else to go to and meet people and lead a much more normal life. Snooker is not a normal life, not just playing it. I think it is one of the most difficult of all sports to cope with. It is a very lonely existence and one of the most demanding.

This was really brought home to me at the beginning of the 1988/89 season. I was up at the Fidelity Unit Trusts International in September, the qualifying section that was. At this stage there are 64 players involved and it is like a travelling circus. There are the newcomers waiting to play their match and they are hanging around in great excitement. Then you turn round and Rex Williams is walking in. He has been competing for 30-odd years and has been through this so many times that he does not give it a thought. In the middle are the players from the fringe who want to be stars but cannot quite make it. But they still pretend to be stars and go through all the motions, like: Why haven't we got a car to take us back to the hotel? Why can't we have steak and chips up here while we're watching the snooker?

Amongst all that is Steve Davis, who is sitting quietly in a corner with his father eating a pack of sandwiches and drinking a cup of tea. There they all were, in one room, the differing faces of snooker.

I had just lost 5–0 to Jimmy Wych and was not in particularly good spirits. It was the first match of the year and I had just been demolished. Steve, in his usual happy-go-lucky way, said: 'What was the score then?' Of course he was expecting me to win. When I told him I had been whitewashed, he did not know what to say. In fact now he did not want to say anything. So I added, 'I played very badly.' By this time he had worked out a suitable reply, which was meant to be comforting but really said nothing at all. 'I lost 5–0 to Ray Reardon last season and was playing great in practice.' The conversation did not go any further because Steve had to go and get ready for his match.

What was significant for me about that incident was that there was the world champion sitting there quietly in jeans and a sweater eating sandwiches he had brought with him. I wondered how many of the younger players trying to get on in the game had taken any notice of that or understood the reasons behind it. Because in many ways it was the perfect object lesson. Steve has always managed to bring himself down to as low a plane as he can. And because he has been much more successful than anybody else on the circuit, I think it is more noticeable. He does not dress up in fancy clothes or run around in fancy cars. I think he purposefully steers away from these things because he does not want to be that type of person or be seen as such. Of course he is the complete showman on the table. He comes to life out there. But off the table, he just wants to be the same as anyone else. In some ways life is easier for him. For a start he is single and can be totally dedicated to snooker. He does not have to sacrifice family life and whatever else he sacrifices does not affect him because he has never had any of it.

I have never managed to do that. Because of my way of life, the type of person I am and the upbringing I have had, I have never got the mix of it quite right. It has either been all glamour or nothing at all. In one way, I have led a very enclosed life and that was one of the reasons why I hated going away on tour so much. I used to dread those trips. I had the chance of spending two or three months at home with the family, relaxing and doing exactly what I wanted, and the next thing I knew I was flying off to the other side of the world for three weeks. Getting the balance right has always been the hardest part. I have never really been able to achieve it and I suppose inevitably did start to resent what I was doing.

Of course the tours were superb in many ways. The organisation was faultless; the money was very good; we always had first-class travel and accommodation and the countries we visited were fascinating. With all that, it is difficult to explain my reactions to people without sounding totally unappreciative. But in many ways those tours have been too much first-class. And there was no break between that and coming back to my normal routine. And it was then that I started looking more closely at myself and wondering what on earth I was doing with my life. Snooker was becoming very much of secondary importance. I was now much more concerned about myself as a person and trying to find out why I was not really happy. On the surface, there was no reason to be unhappy. I have a wonderful family and a very good way of life. But those things can very often hide the truth. Because I was so comfortable, I was probably beginning to react against it.

The last week of the 1985 Far East Tour, when we were in Hong Kong, was almost certainly one of the worst weeks of my life. I just could not accept being there; I could not accept myself as a person; the other players were getting on my nerves; everything was getting me down and literally I was a pain in the backside to everyone around me. I used to disappear off to my room, lock the door and read a book. But then I won the tournament in Hong Kong.

I have found the balance of being a normal person in such a situation to be virtually impossible to achieve. And that makes life very hard.

It is at times like this that you always feel the grass is greener on the other side. When I hear friends of mine at home complaining about having to get up in the morning to go to work, I often think how nice that would be, having a normal everyday job again.

201

There has been many a time when I have prayed for that, although deep down I know I could never cope with it again.

I am very much the sort of person who looks inside, rather than outside, for the solution to problems. Naturally on the circuit you spend a lot of time by yourself, often just sitting in a hotel room, and it is then that I think about why I feel the way I do. I try to be as truthful as I can with myself and to appreciate how lucky I am to be gifted enough to play professional snooker. The club and the house have helped me understand how fortunate I have been. Those months I spent working with the lads reminded me of how other people's lives are limited by what they do. Yet somehow they have got peace of mind. And that is one thing I envy them for. I know I do not get peace of mind out of being a professional snooker player. I never have – not even in victory. But, there again, defeats have never really hit me hard, either.

At the end of the day, however, snooker is the life I chose, and I must accept it for what it is.